Foreword

○ **Hawker Hurricane PR Mk I, P2638, No.208 (Army Co-operation) Squadron, Burg-el-Arab, Egypt, 1942**
Dark Earth/Mid Stone/Azure Blue finish with black spinner and serial; White flash flanking fuselage roundel. Squiggle type mottling on nose and wing leading edges; standard national markings. This unarmed reconnaissance aircraft was shot down by Bf 109Fs on 24th July 1942

Airframe Extra No.9
The North African Campaign – 10th June 1940 to the 13th May 1943

First published in 2018 by Valiant Wings Publishing Ltd
8 West Grove, Bedford, Bedfordshire, MK40 4BT, UK
+44 (0)1234 273434
valiant-wings@btconnect.com
www.valiant-wings.co.uk

© Patrick Branly – Historical Introduction
© Richard J. Caruana – Colour Profiles
© Steve A. Evans (Section 2)
© Libor Jekl (Section 2)

The 'Airframe Extra' brand, along with the concept of the series, are the copyright of Richard A. Franks as defined by the Copyright Designs and Patents Act, 1988 and are used by Valiant Wings Publishing Ltd by agreement with the copyright holder.

All rights reserved. No part of this publication may be reproduced or transmitted in any form or by any means, electronic or mechanical, including photocopy, recording, or any other information storage and retrieval system, without permission in writing from the publishers.

ISBN: 978-0-9957773-2-3

Acknowledgements
The publishers would like to give a special word of thanks to Steve A. Evans and Libor Jekl for their excellent builds featured in this special, and to Jerry Boucher and Richard J. Caruana for their superb artwork.

Note
To put the air war over North Africa in context, the accompanying narrative looks in detail at the offensive on the ground, as most operations in the theatre at this time were in direct support of the ground forces.

Cover
The cover art depicts Tomahawk Mk IIs from No.112 Squadron in combat with Axis aircraft during late November 1941. This artwork was specially commissioned for this title ©Jerry Boucher 2018

Welcome to our ninth Airframe Extra title. This time we are rolling the clock back from our previous title on the air war over Italy to the North African Campaign which provided the springboard to later campaigns in Sicily and Italy.

The desert was probably made for war and favoured neither side. Vast expanses of arid landscape challenged navigational skills. Extreme heat and cold and upper air temperatures altered aircraft performances from their normal European environments. Sand played havoc with moving parts and was the enemy of aircraft engines. Any slip or lack of concentration in navigation or fuel level reading could ultimately be fatal as much as being shot down in combat. The potential for the former is well documented in Roald Dahl's 'Solo'. It's a good read.

The North Africa Campaign threw up new challenges for aircraft engineers as they devised new engine sand filters to avoid their charges being grounded. The conflict spawned new varieties of concealment camouflage. European greens gave way to sand and brown to better blend in with operating environments. This transition has been captured very well by Richard Caruana's special set of profiles commissioned for this title. The amount available is bewildering and we had quite a challenge striking the right balance so that all the protagonists were properly represented. We hope that we've done them justice.

Patrick Branly has pulled out all the stops and described the ebb and flow of the conflict in his usual excellent style. For those of you with an interest in modelling the period Steve Evans and Libor Jekl have produced some wonderful examples of modelling skills in four different scales. Both 1/32 and 1/144 scales are growing in popularity so we haven't forgotten either in this title. All the builds are eye-poppingly superb but Steve's Ju 52 is just exquisite.

We hope that you enjoy this latest Airframe Extra. It's a bit of a milestone for us as it is our 41st title in under eight years. Many thanks for helping us get there.

Mark Peacock – *Publisher*

Content

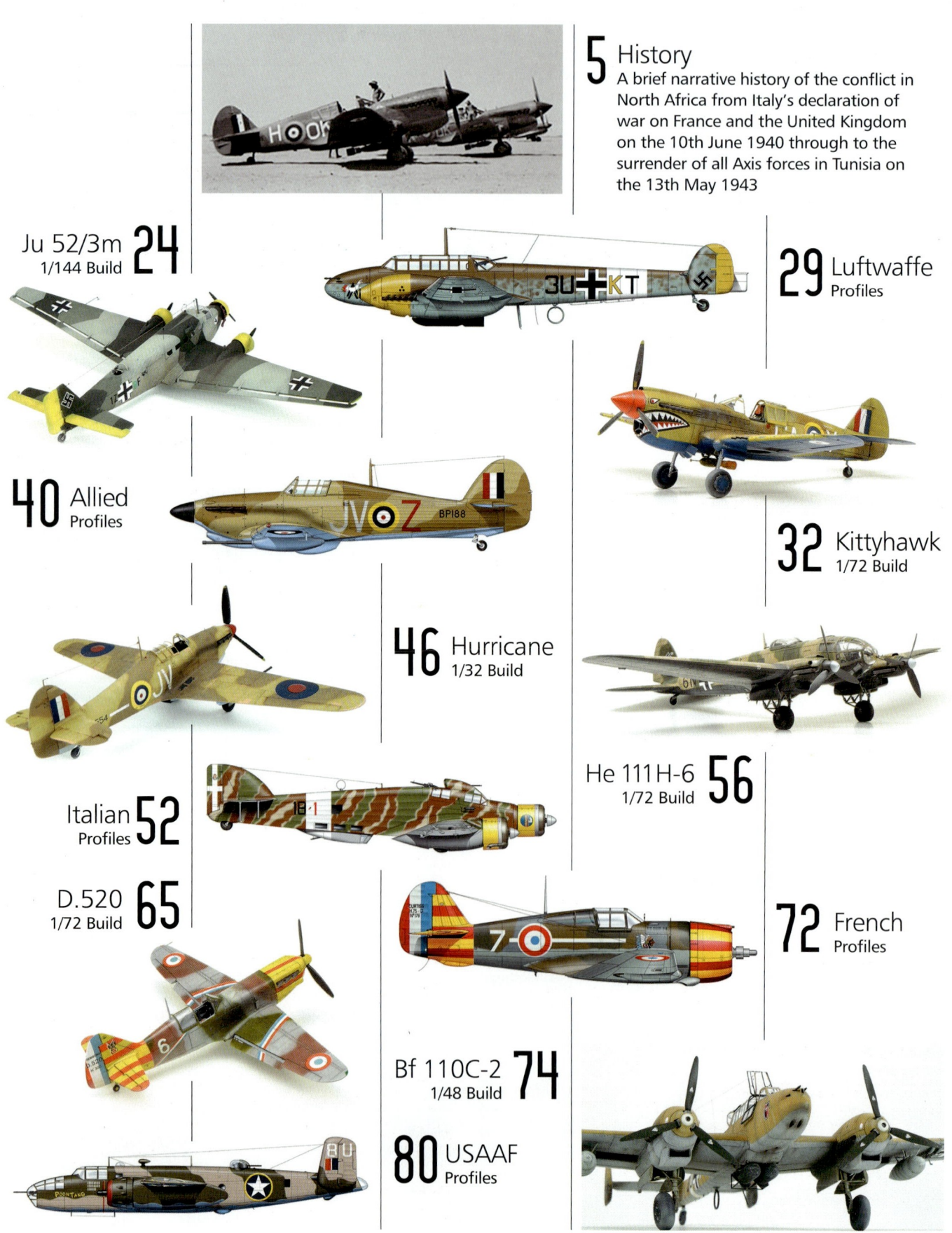

5 History
A brief narrative history of the conflict in North Africa from Italy's declaration of war on France and the United Kingdom on the 10th June 1940 through to the surrender of all Axis forces in Tunisia on the 13th May 1943

Ju 52/3m **24**
1/144 Build

29 Luftwaffe Profiles

40 Allied Profiles

32 Kittyhawk
1/72 Build

46 Hurricane
1/32 Build

He 111 H-6 **56**
1/72 Build

Italian Profiles **52**

D.520 **65**
1/72 Build

72 French Profiles

Bf 110C-2 **74**
1/48 Build

80 USAAF Profiles

History

On 3rd September 1939, when Great Britain and France declared war against the Third Reich, Italy avoided getting involved in the European conflict. When the Nazi armed forces gained many victories in Poland, Norway, Belgium, The Netherlands and France, Benito Mussolini decided that Fascist Italy was to be more than a partner of Nazi Germany and declared war against Great Britain and France on 10th June 1940. After some short periods of fighting in southern France the main front for the Italian armed forces therefore became North Africa.

1940
& Operation Compass

When Maréchal Pétain signed an armistice with Germany on 22nd June 1940, France kept control of their territories in North Africa, that is to say the Moroccan and Tunisian Protectorates and

French Algeria. Since the Italian-Turkish War in 1911-1912 Italy had gained territories in North Africa (modern day Libya). These territories were divided into three areas: Tripolitania on the western shore of the Mediterranean Sea with Tripoli as the main town; Cyrenaica on the eastern shore around the city of Benghazi; and a large area of the Saharan Desert called the *Fezzan*. Nonetheless Benito Mussolini was ultimately setting his sights on Egypt, the Nile and the Suez Canal.

Order of Battle on 10th June 1940

Italian Armed Forces in North Africa
under the Command of Maresciallo dell'Aria Italo Balbo
- **5th Army on the western border facing French Tunisia**
- X Corpo with the 25th Infantry Division '*Bologna*' and the 60th Infantry Division '*Sabratha*'
- XX Corpo with the 17th Infantry Division '*Pavia*', the 61st Infantry Division '*Sirte*' and the 27th Infantry Division '*Brescia*'

Armourers of No.113 Squadron place 20lb fragmentation bombs into small bomb containers for loading into a Bristol Blenheim Mk I at Ma'aten Bagush, Egypt (©Imperial War Museum)

by Patrick Branly

- XXIII Corpo with the 1st Blackshirt Division '*23 Marzo*', the 2nd Blackshirt Division '*28 Ottobre*' and the 2nd Libyan Division '*Pescatore*'

- **10th Army on the eastern border facing British forces in Egypt**
- XXI Corpo with the 63rd Infantry Division '*Cirene*' and the 62nd Infantry Division '*Marmarica*'
- XXII Corpo with the 64th Infantry Division '*Catanzaro*', the 4th Blackshirt Division '*3 Gennaio*' and the 1st Libyan Division '*Sibelle*'
- **Generale di Squadra Aerea (Air Marshal) Felice Porro's 5a Squadra Aerea della Libia comprising:**
Bombers and strike aircraft:
- 10° Stormo B.T. (*Bombardamento Terrestre*) with Savoia-Marchetti S.79
- 14° Stormo B.T. with Savoia-Marchetti S.79 & S.81
- 15° Stormo B.T. with Savoia-Marchetti S.79 & S.81
- 33° Stormo B.T. with Savoia-Marchetti S.79
- 50° Stormo Ass. (*Assalto*) with Caproni Ca.310 & Breda Ba.65
- 1st and 2nd A.P.C. (*Aviazione di Presidio Coloniale*) with Caproni Ca.309

Fighters:
- 8° Gruppo C.T. (*Caccia Terrestre*) with Fiat CR.42
- 10° Gruppo C.T. with Fiat CR.42
- 13° Gruppo C.T. with Fiat CR.32/42

Reconnaissance:
- 64° O.A. (*Osservazione Aerea*) with IMAM Ro.37
- 73° O.A. with IMAM Ro.37

Officers of the 11th Hussars in a Morris CS9 armoured car using a parasol to good effect near the Libyan border on the 26th July 1940 (©Imperial War Museum)

10/06/1940 to 07/02/1941

The Savoia-Marchetti S.79 bomber was powered by three 860hp Alfa 128 R.C.18 radial engines with a crew of six and capable of reaching a maximum speed of 286mph with a maximum load of 2,645lb of bombs. It could also deliver a couple of 450mm torpedoes, which were carried under the fuselage/wings. Its maiden flight took place on the 28th September 1934, it had a wingspan of 66ft 3in, a length of 53ft 2in and the *Spavierro* (Sparrowhawk) had a range of 1,615 miles.

The Fiat CR.32 was a streamlined biplane fighter built with aluminium and steel tubing and covered with aluminium sheets from the nose to the cockpit with fabric covering the remainder. It was powered by a 600hp Fiat A30 RA-bis V12 engine and could fly at a maximum speed of 224mph. It was armed with a couple of 0.50in Breda-SAFAT machine-guns and had a wingspan of 31ft 2 1/4in and a length of 24ft 6in.

The Fiat CR.42 Falco (Falcon), the last biplane fighter operated by the *Regia Aeronautica*, made its first flight on 23rd May 1938 and was powered by a Fiat A.74 radial air-cooled fourteen-cylinder engine delivering 840hp. With this engine the CR.42 had a maximum speed of 274mph and was armed with up to four 0.50in machine-guns. The CR.42 was almost a sesquiplane with the upper wing of 31ft 10in span and the lower of 21ft 4in and an overall length of 27ft 1in.

The IMAM (*Industrie Meccaniche Aeronautiche Meridionali*) Ro.37 Lince (Lynx) was an observation biplane aircraft that first flew on the 6th November 1933 and with a crew of two could fly with a maximum speed of 205mph. Powered by a 560hp nine-cylinder air-cooled Piaggio P.IX radial engine, it had a wingspan of 36ft 4in, an overall length of 28ft 1in and a range of 700 miles. It was armed with three 0.303in machine-guns, one of which was on a flexible mount in the rear cockpit for defensive purposes.

British and Commonwealth Armed Forces in Middle East

under the Command of General Sir Archibald Wavell
- 7th Armoured Division with the 4th Armoured Brigade at Mersa Matruh and a Motorized Infantry Brigade at Sidi Barrani
- 4th Indian Division with the 5th and 11th Indian Infantry Brigades
- 6th Australian Division in the Nile Delta
- 2nd New Zealand Division in the Nile Delta
- 202nd Group, RAF included:
  - 250 (Bomber) Wing with Nos.30, 55 and 113 Squadrons operating the Bristol Blenheim
  - 251 (Bomber) Wing with Nos.70 and 216 Squadrons flying the Vickers Wellington and Bristol Bombay
  - 252 (Fighter) Wing with Nos.80 and 112 Squadrons along with Nos.2 and 5 Squadrons, Royal Egyptian Air Force all operating the Gloster Gladiator
  - 253 Wing with No.33 Squadron operating the Gloster Gladiator, Nos.45 and 211 using the Bristol Blenheim and No.208 flying the Westland Lysander

The first shots of what is called the Western Desert War started at dawn on 11th June 1940, when six Rolls-Royce armoured cars from platoons of 11th Hussar crossed the 'Wire', the Egyptian-Libyan border, for an armed reconnaissance of the Italian positions at Fort Capuzzo and

Mk VIb light tanks of the 7th Armoured Division on patrol in the Desert on the 2nd August 1940
(©Imperial War Museum)

Fort Maddalena. On the 14th June a stronger operation involved a 4th Armoured Brigade assault on Fort Cappuzzo near the Mediterranean coastline and Sidi Azeiz to prevent any reinforcement of the fort. After taking the fort without any casualties on either side the British forces captured twenty-six Italian officers and soldiers and 200 Libyan soldiers. There were some casualties during the fighting around Sidi Azeiz however and when the British forces went back behind the 'Wire' they destroyed Fort Capuzzo. After these first shots the 7th Armoured Division forces consolidated their positions to observe the Italian movements and prepare themselves to strike back at any Italian invasion of Egypt.

The Italian Invasion of Egypt (Operazione E)

After the initial skirmishes along the 'Wire' Italian forces had been reinforced since the French armistice on the 24th June effectively getting rid of any threat from the Tunisian border. In order to prepare an invasion of Egypt the Italian Armed Forces transferred two Corps to Generale d'Armata Italo Gariboldi's 10th Army. On the eve of the invasion in early September 1940, the 10th Army included XX, XXI, XXII and XXIII Corps.

On the 13th September 1940, the men of the 1st Blackshirt Division '23 Marzo' occupied Fort Capuzzo and crossed the Egyptian border. With four divisions and 300 aircraft the Italian forces had the edge over the British, and after four days of fighting the Italians halted and entrenched east of the village of Sidi Barani, the farthest point of their 100km advance. Once again the war became a static one due to the limited goals of the Italian offensive. For the months to come General Wavell's forces were strengthened in order to prepare a counter-offensive.

Fiat CR.42s of 73a and 96a Squadriglia, 9° Gruppo, Benina, Libya in 1940 (©Italian Air Force)

Operation Compass

Now facing the British and Commonwealth forces the Italian 10th Army had three corps in the frontline with XXI Corps being placed as a reserve force in Cyrenaica and XXII & XIII Corps on the frontline itself. On the other side the Western Desert Force, a reinforced force of corps size, under the command of Lieutenant-General R. N. O'Connor, was made up of Major-General M. O'Moore Creagh's 7th Armoured Division (4th & 7th Armoured Brigades, Support Group and Divisional Troops), Major-General N.M. De la P. Beresford-Peirse's 4th Indian Division (5th & 11th Indian Infantry Brigades, 16th British Infantry Brigade and Divisional Troops), Brigadier A.R. Selby's, Selby Force from Mersa Matruh garrison and artillery and the 7th Royal Tank Regiment attached to the corps. Above them 202 Group would provide air cover with Nos.45, 55 & 113 Squadrons (flying the Bristol Blenheim), Nos.33 & 274 Squadrons (flying the Hawker Hurricane), No.3 RAAF Squadron (flying the Gloster Gladiator) and Nos.6 & 208 Army Co-Operation Squadrons (operating the Hawker Hurricane and Westland Lysander).

Operation Compass, the Allied counter-offensive, started on the 8th December 1940 with a naval bombardment and on the 10th the village of Sidi Barrani was re-taken by elements of the 16th British Infantry Brigade and the 7th Royal Tank Regiment. The next day the 4th Indian Infantry Division, less the 16th Brigade, had to move to Sudan and was replaced by Major-General L.G. Mckay's 6th Australian Division (16th, 17th & 19th Australian Infantry Brigades and Divisional Artillery and troops). By the evening of the 12th December Allied troops reached the 'Wire', thus liberating Egyptian territory. After seizing Fort Capuzzo and Sollum they had 38,300

prisoners, 237 guns, 73 tanks and 1,000 vehicles for a cost of 624 casualties. The Italian forces suffered 2,300 servicemen killed and the same number were wounded.

With this victory General Wavell decided to exploit the situation and on the 3rd January 1941 the next move was made in the direction of Bardia, the first city on the Cyrenaica coastline. After three days of fighting the Allies, essentially Australian forces under Major-General L.G. Mackay, captured Bardia and 36,000 Italian soldiers. The next move was in the direction of Tobruk, an important harbour on the Mediterranean. The Western Desert Force (renamed since the 1st January as XIII Corps) reached the first positions around Tobruk on the 7th January. The assault started on the 21st January and the next day British and Australian forces took the port of Tobruk and received the surrender from Admiral Massimiliano Vietina of the *Regia Marina* garrison. In that battle the Allied forces captured another 20,000 soldiers, 208 guns and 87 tanks for the loss of 400 men.

As was nearly always the case during the Western Desert Campaign the action followed the coastline with only occasional moves inland to go round enemy positions, and in this instance the movement was westward. The 6th Australian Division headed towards Derna on the coastline and the 7th British Armoured Division advanced in the direction of Mechili, which they entered on the 27th January. Derna and its airfield were taken on the 29th January.

To secure the flanks of the Allied front, there were a couple of offensives into the desert. First the 6th Australian Divisional Cavalry Regiment undertook an ultimately victorious siege of Jiaradub, some 200 miles south of Bardia and the Italian garrison there surrendered on the 21st

Savoia-Marchetti S.79s of 193a Squadriglia, 87° Gruppo (©Andrea Nicola & Italian Wikipedia)

A Rolls-Royce armoured car passing through the Italian barbed wire on the Egyptian-Libyan border on the 26th July 1940 (©Imperial War Museum)

March 1941. At the same time 350 men of the Free French Troop and the 76 men of the Long Range Desert Group achieved the surrender of the Italian garrison at Kufra Oasis after fighting from the 31st January to the 1st March 1941. The last units of the Italian 10th Army were retreating along the Via Balba through the Cyrenaica capital of Benghazi. To destroy them the 6th Australian Division ran along the Via Balba too and entered Barce, north of Benghazi, on the 5th February. In the meantime the 7th British Armoured Division captured Beda Fomm preparing to surround the Italian 10th Army. Putting an end to Operation Compass on 7th February 1941, the trapped Italian forces surrendered and only a couple of thousand soldiers managed to escape to Tripolitania. In all the Italian Forces lost 133,300 soldiers taken prisoner, 420 tanks and 845 guns. It was a complete disaster for Fascist Italy and a matter of concern for Nazi Germany.

One key element of the success of the Allied forces was what we now call interdiction missions. The Italian forces relied on supplies from the mainland through naval convoys crossing the Mediterranean and lorries running along the Tripolitania coastline roads. At sea the Italian supply lines were attacked by bomber squadrons stationed on Malta, while the road convoys were bombed by the units of the 202nd Group, for which the group relied on the Bristol Blenheim with fighter protection provided by Hawker Hurricane and Gloster Gladiator squadrons. The

Bristol Blenheim (See Airframe Album No.5, ISBN: 978-0-9575866-5-9 ©2014) was a light bomber, developed from a civil airliner, which first flew on the 12th April 1935. The main production variants were the Mk I and Mk IV. The latter had a maximum speed of 266mph and could carry up to 1,200lb of bombs. With a wingspan of 56ft 4in and a length of 42ft 7in, the type had a crew of three and was powered by two 920hp Bristol Mercury XV radial engines giving it a range of 1,640 miles. The Desert War saw the last biplane fighters in combat and the Gloster Gladiator (See Airframe Album No.12, ISBN: 978-0-9957773-1-6 ©2017) proved to be a strong opponent for the Italian fighters. The Gladiator first flew on the 12th September 1934 and was armed with four 0.303in machine-guns. With a span of 32ft 3in and a length of 27ft 5in it had a top speed of 253mph. With a service ceiling of 32,800ft the Gladiator was a very agile and efficient aircraft in the hands of seasoned pilots. The Hawker Hurricane was, at the time, the most modern aircraft operated by the Royal Air Force in the Western Desert. It first flew on the 6th November 1935 and it was faster and stronger than the last biplane fighters of both the RAF and the *Regia Aeronautica*. The Mk I was powered by a 1,030hp V-12 liquid-cooled Rolls-Royce Merlin, with eight 0.303in machine-guns, a top speed of 340mph, a wingspan of 40ft and length of 31ft 9in.

1941

Enter the Deutsches Afrika Korps

Operation Sonnenblume

Adolf Hitler could not accept that his Italian allies had lost possession of territory in North Africa, even when his own expansionist plans were looking east to Russian at the time. He therefore set-up *Operation Sonnenblume* (Operation Sunflower) to dispatch to North Africa a *Kampfgruppe* and the first elements crossed the Mediterranean on the 11th February 1941. The new *Deutsches Afrika Korps* (DAK) as it was named had been created by the German High Command (*Oberkommando der Wehrmacht* – OKW) to act as a blocking force in Tripolitania and thence secure the Axis presence in North Africa.

Armourers working on a Curtiss Tomahawk of an RAAF Squadron on the 23rd December 1941
(©Australian War Memorial)

Savoia-Marchetti SM.82 Marsupiale MM.60279 from 604a Squadriglia, 145º Gruppo
(via Wikimedia Commons)

The DAK

under the command of *Generalleutnant* Erwin Rommel, which was officially formed on 19th February 1941, included on paper at least:
- Generalmajor Johan Streich's 5th Light Afrika Division, to become later that year the 21st Panzer Division
- Generalmajor Karl Freiherr von Esebeck's 15th Panzer Division
- 5th Panzer Regiment, the core of the 5th Light Division was finally equipped on African soil on the 11th March

The DAK was reinforced with the Italian XX Corps' divisions:
- Generale di Brigata Antonio Franceschini's 17th Infantry Division '*Pavia*'
- Generale di Divizione Bortolo Zambone's 27th Infantry Division '*Brescia*'
- Generale di Divizione Mario Balotta's 132nd Armoured Division '*Ariete*'

The Allied Forces (in Cyrenaica)

had changed due to British involvement in the defence of Greece, so ranged against the DAK were the following recently formed divisions:
- Major-General M.D. Gambier-Parry's 2nd British Armoured Division
- Major-General L.J. Morshead's 9th Australian Infantry Division
- Brigadier E.W.D. Vaughn's 3rd Indian (Motor) Brigade

On 24th March 1941, the first panzer elements of the DAK moved towards the British positions south-east of Mersa Brega and the offensive started on the 1st April. They reached Agedabia on the 3rd April as the British forces retreated along the Via Balba as their Italian counterparts had done the previous January. The two Italian Infantry Divisions secured the areas after the breakthrough of the 5th Panzer Regiment. As the first units of the DAK reached Benghazi they were divided in two columns, one following the Via Balba to Barce and the other one towards Mechilli. By the 6th April the Germans turned to the east of Derna thus closing one route of retreat for the Allied forces along the Via Balba. After the attack on Mechilli the British forces retreated to El Adem but after fierce fighting on the 8th April Major-General M.D. Gambier-Parry and roughly 3,000 British soldiers surrendered to the commander of the 17th Infantry Division '*Pavia*'.

By the 11th April the city and the harbour of Tobruk were surrounded by DAK forces with the 5th Light Panzer Division on the east side. With about 25,000 soldiers the garrison of Tobruk would be a dangerous stronghold and prevented the movement of the Italian-German forces that wanted to invade Egypt. Furthermore the British and Australian troops were well equipped and could be replenished by sea thanks to the Royal

Naval fleet based in Alexandria. The 11th April marked the start of a 142-day siege until the Allies finally broke through to Tobruk later in the year. The DAK forces however had to wait for supplies coming from Benghazi some 560 mile away on the Egyptian border. By the end of April DAK forces, after a fortnight of hard fighting

to seize Tobruk, which they failed to do, settled along the Egyptian border just as the Italian forces had at the beginning of the Western Desert War in June 1940. The main difference now though was the trouble-spot that was Tobruk.

Operation Brevity

The first attempt by the Allies to counter-attack was a limited offensive commencing on the 15th May 1941 and called Operation Brevity. Actually, General Sir Archibald Wavell defined Operation Brevity as a means to gain some territories to prepare a stronger offensive in order to relieve Tobruk. British forces under the command of Brigadier William Gott were mainly the 7th Armoured Brigade Group and the 22nd Guards Brigade Group and there were three prongs to this offensive. On the 15th May 1941 the centre column with the 22nd Guards Brigade Group reached the top of the Halfaya Pass, while the desert column with the 7th Armoured Brigade Group advanced towards Fort Capuzzo and the coastline column with the remaining British forces fighting hard to get to the bottom of the Halfaya Pass. Fierce resistance by the Italian and German forces brought the offensive to a

Painting the engine cowl on a Messerschnmitt Bf 109E of JG27 in North Africa in 1941
(©German Federal Archives)

A Messerschmitt Me 323 Gigant landing on an airfield somewhere in North Africa in 1941
(©German Federal Archives)

halt just a day later. Actually the main gain of Operation Brevity was the seizing of the Halfaya Pass, which could have been a real bonus for the offensives to come. That's why on the 26th May the Axis Forces under Colonel Maximillian von Herff launched *Operation Skorpion* to retake the Halfaya Pass. It was a success and the situation for the Allied forces went back to the one that had existed before Brevity.

Operation Battleaxe

The next Allied move would be on a larger scale and had the aim of repelling the Axis forces out of Cyrenaica. At the time there were good and bad points due to the loss of the Greek island of Crete. This meant that some British troops came back under Middle East Command but on the other hand the Germans could use new airfields from the island to strike the Egyptian positions. The Allied forces were formed around Lieutenant-General N.M. De la P. Beresford-Peirse's XIII Corps with Major-General M. O'Moore Creagh's 7th Armoured Division (4th & 7th Armoured Brigades, Support Group and Divisional Troops) and Major-General F.W. Messervy's 4th Indian Division (11th Indian Infantry Brigade, 22th British Guards

Infantry Brigade and Divisional Troops). But the Germans had been reinforced too with the arrival of 100 tanks of the 15th Panzer Division along the border. At 6.00am on the 16th June 1941, Matilda tanks of the 4th Royal Tank Regiment started moving towards the Halfaya Pass but without good artillery support they were nearly annihilated by the 88mm anti-tank guns of Major Wilhelm Bach, and the same fate awaited the Cameroons of the 11th Indian Infantry Brigade who started their offensive at 10.00am. The 7th Royal Tank Regiment advance was much more efficient when they crossed the 'Wire' and attacked Fort Capuzzo. The 7th Armoured Brigade (2nd and 6th Royal Tank Regiments) and the 22nd Guards Brigade after an easy start to the day had to retreat due to a strong counter-attack by German forces, losing over half of their tanks in the process. The next day the German counter-offensive was stronger with the 5th Light Panzer Division making an encircling manoeuvre in the desert and it was only because of both British Division commanders' decision to retreat quickly that the Allied forces were not surrounded and destroyed. The British lost around 100 tanks during Operation Battleaxe and even if the Axis forces lost 50, they held the terrain after the battle so could recover and repair most of them so that in the end only 12 were totally written off. After yet another failure the British Prime Minister was no longer satisfied with the leadership of General Sir Archibald Wavell, so he was replaced by General Sir Claude Auchinleck.

Operation Crusader

After the near disaster of Operation Battleaxe the new Commander-in-Chief Middle East Command General Sir Claude Auchinleck decided to wait for the arrival of more troops and the end of the hot summer season before preparing another offensive to relieve the defenders of Tobruk. At the beginning of November 1941 before Operation Crusader commenced the order of battle was as follows:

Allied forces
under Middle-East Command:
- **Lieutenant-General Allan Cunningham's British 8th Army comprising:**
- Lieutenant-General Willoughby Norrie's XXX Corps
- Major-General William Gott's 7th Armoured Division (4th, 7th and 22nd Armoured Brigades, Support and Divisional troops)
- Major-General George Brink's 1st South African Division (1st and 5th South African Infantry Brigades) and the British 22nd Guards Brigade
- Lieutenant-General Reade Godwin-Austen's XIII Corps comprising:
   - Major-General's 2nd New-Zealand Infantry Division (4th, 5th and 6th New-Zealand Infantry Brigades)
   - Major-General Frank Messervy's 4th Indian Infantry Division (5th, 7th and 11th Indian Infantry Brigades and Divisional troops) and the 1st Army Tank Brigade (8th, 42nd and 44th Royal Tank Regiments)
   - Major-General Isaac de Villiers' 2nd South-African Infantry Division (3rd, 4th and 6th South-African Infantry Brigades) held as an Army reserve
- Major-General Ronald Scobie's Tobruk fortress containing:
   - 70th Infantry Division (14th, 16th and 23rd Infantry Brigades)
   - Polish Independent Carpathian Rifle Brigade
   - 32nd Army Tank Brigade (1st, 4th and D Squadron 7th RTR)

Groundcrew performing maintenance on the engine of a Junkers Ju 87B/R in North Afrika in 1941
(©German Federal Archives)

Axis Forces
under the Supreme Commander North Africa, Generale di Armata Ettore Bastico
- **Generalleutnant Erwin Rommel's Panzer-Gruppe Afrika:**
- *Generalleutnant* Ludwig Crüwell's *Deutches Afrika Korps*
- *Generalmajor* Walter Neumann-Silkow's 15th Panzer Division (8th Panzer Regiment, 115th Infantry Regiment and Divisional troops)
- *Generalmajor* Johann von Ravenstein's 21st Panzer Division (5th Panzer Regiment, 104th Infantry Regiment and Divisional Troops)
- *Generalmajor* Max Sümmermann's 90th *Leichte Afrika* Infantry Division and Generale di Divizione Fedele de Giorsis' 55th Infantry Division 'Savona'
- *Generale di Corpo d'Armata* Enea Navarini's Italian XXI Corps with 17th Infantry Division 'Pavia', 25th Infantry Division 'Bologna', 27th Infantry Division 'Brescia' and 102nd Motorized Division 'Trento'
- **Generale di Corpo d'Armata Gastone Gambara's Italian XX Corps (Mobile Corps)**
- 132nd Armoured Division 'Ariete'
- 101st Motorised Division 'Trieste'

British troops inspect a Junkers Ju 87B-2 of 5./StG2 that had landed in the desert in December 1941 (©Imperial War Museum)

Just before dawn on the 18th November 1941, the 8th Army advanced westwards from their base at Mersa Matruh and crossed the Libyan border seizing Fort Maddalena. Even if these first moves went well the Italian Division 'Ariete' stopped the 22nd Armoured Brigade at Bir El Gubi jeopardizing 7th Armoured Brigade's flank. From the 21st November, 70th Infantry Division attacked from their position in Tobruk to meet up with the 7th Armoured Brigade advance, but failed. On the 23rd November during the battle of Sidi Rezegh the South Africans of the 3rd Field Artillery managed to block a German counter-offensive; they were all wiped out but their sacrifice constituted the turning point

Martin Maryland Mk II, No.1655 of the South African Air Force being refuelled at Ma'aten Bagush, Egypt
(©Imperial War Museum)

A Matilda tank around Tobruk displaying an Italian flag as a war trophy on the 24th January 1941
(©Imperial War Museum)

of Operation Crusader as the same day the 5th New Zealand Brigade cut off the Italian/German positions between Sidi Omar and Sollum. On the 25th November Rommel's new attack this time was blocked and after fierce fighting a corridor was created to Tobruk on the 27th November. That day General Auchinleck replaced Lieutenant-General Allan Cunningham at the head of British 8th Army with Major-General Neil Ritchie. Between the 4th and 7th December another battle was fought at Bir el Gubi but this time the XXX Corps won and then the DAK had to retreat up to the Gazala Line. It was just a temporary halt as Italian and German forces did not receive enough supplies to hold the line and on the 16th December they retreated westwards, again to form a strong defence line at El Agheila in Tripolitania by the 27th December.

This meant that by the end of 1941 the Italian and German ground forces were back at their initial positions when they launched *Operation Sonnenblume* on the 24th March that year.

During this year of intense fighting the air forces of both sides had increased in both quality and quantity. Just before the launch of *Opera-*

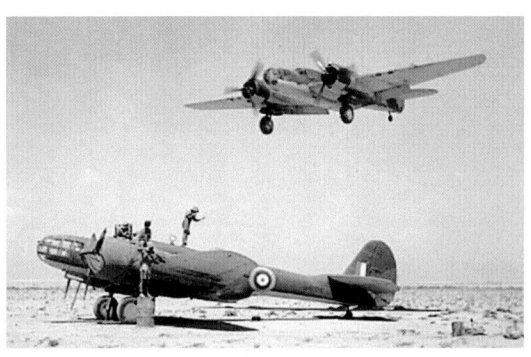

tion Crusader the fighter wings were reorganized by creating wings of the same type of aircraft and the Western Desert Air Force was organized mainly as follows.
- No 262 (Fighter) Wing with the Hawker Hurricane included Nos.1 (SAAF), 94, 229, 238, 260 and 274 Squadrons
- No 258 (Fighter) Wing with the Curtiss Tomahawk included Nos.2 (SAAF), 3 (RAAF), 4 (SAAF), 112, 250 and the Royal Navy Squadrons. Nos.30 and 80 Squadrons reported directly to Western Desert Air Force HQ
- No 253 (Army Co-operation) Wing with the Hawker Hurricane included Nos.208, 237 and 451 Squadrons.
- No.3, SAAF (Medium Bomber) Wing operating the Martin Maryland included Nos.12, 21 & 24 SAAF Squadrons and No.11 Squadron (RAF) using the Bristol Blenheim
- No.270 (Medium Bomber) Wing with the Bristol Blenheim included Nos.8, 14, 45, 55, 84 and Free French 'Lorraine' Squadrons

On the other side the *Regia Aeronautica* had the following order of battle operating behind the 'Wire'.
- *Commando Settore Ovest* (Tripoli) with 98° Gruppo B.T. (*Bombardamento Terrestre*) With the Fiat BR.20, 3° Gruppo C.T. (*Caccia Terrestre*) with the Fiat CR.42, 12° Gruppo C.T. (*Caccia*

Flight Lieutenant D. S. G. Honor in front of a No.274 Squadron Hawker Hurricane
(©Imperial War Museum)

Terrestre) with the Fiat G.50 and 145° Gruppo Trasporti operating the Savoia-Marchetti S.74/75 and S.82
- *Commando Settore Centrale* (Benghazi) with 160° Gruppo C.T. (*Caccia Terrestre*) flying the Fiat CR.42, 360a Squadriglia C.T. (*Caccia Terrestre*) using the Fiat G.50, 244a Squadriglia B.T. (*Bombardamento Terrestre*) operating the Savoia-Marchetti S.81 and 209a Squadriglia Ba.T. (*Bombardamento a Tuffo*) with the Junkers Ju 87
- *Commando Settore Est* (Derna) with 13° Stormo B.T. (*Bombardamento Terrestre*) using the Fiat BR.20, 8° Stormo B.T. (*Bombardamento Terrestre*) flying the Savoia-Marchetti S.79, 153° Gruppo C.T. (*Caccia Terrestre*) with the Macchi MC.200 and 155° Gruppo C.T. (*Caccia Terrestre*) using the Fiat G.50

By the 25th November these were reinforced with 9°, 17° & 8° Gruppo C.T. (*Caccia Terrestre*) operating the Macchi MC.202, 151° Gruppo C.T. (*Caccia Terrestre*) with the Fiat CR.42 and 157° Gruppo C.T. (*Caccia Terrestre*) flying the Macchi MC.200. Lastly, December saw the arrival of 150° Gruppo C.T. (*Caccia Terrestre*) with their Macchi MC.200s and 6° Gruppo C.T. (*Caccia Terrestre*) flying the Macchi MC.202.

Martin Maryland Mk II, AH284 of No.39 Squadron in the desert in 1941
(©Imperial War Museum)

Armourers loading 250lb bombs into a Martin Maryland of No.39 Squadron in 1941
(©Imperial War Museum)

A British Crusader tank passing by a burning German tank on the 27th November 1941
(©Imperial War Museum)

Finally, the German Luftwaffe had the following units:
- Stab, I, II and III./JG 27 (*Jagdgeschwader*) and Stab, I, II, III./JG 53 using the Messerschmitt Bf 109F
- I./NJG 2 (*Nacht Jagdgeschwader*) operating the Junkers Ju 88C
- I./StG 1, II./StG 2, Stab and I./StG 3 (*Stuka Geschwader*) flying the Junkers Ju 87
- III./ZG 26 (*Zerstörer Geschwader*) using the Messerschmitt Bf 110
- Stab, I, II and III./LG 1 (*Lehr Geschwader*) with the Junkers Ju 88A
- II./KG 26 (*Kampf Geschwader*) using the Heinkel He 111
- KGr 606 and 806 (*Kampf Gruppe*) operating the Junkers Ju 88A

The Martin Maryland Mk I (Model 167) first flew on the 14th March 1939, and was powered by two 950hp Wright radial engines giving it a maximum speed of 304mph. With a crew of three it was used during the French Campaign as a bomber even if it was usually listed as being a reconnaissance aircraft. The armament comprised four 0.303in Browning machine guns in the wing leading edge and a single 0.303in Vickers K in a cupola above the fuselage and in a recessed hatch underneath. With a wingspan of 61ft 4in and a length of 46ft 8in it could carry 2,000lb of bombs with a maximum range of 1,300 miles.

The Junkers Ju 87, the iconic aircraft of the Blitzkrieg, made its maiden flight on the 17th September 1935 and with a two-man crew could carry 500kg of bombs with a range of 311 miles and a maximum speed of 242mph. It was 36ft 1in long, had a wingspan of 45ft 3 1/3in and was powered by a 1,184hp inverted V-12 liquid-cooled Jumo 211 engine.

The Heinkel He 111 bomber first flew on the 24th February 1935 and had a wingspan of 74ft

Groundcrew performing maintenance on Hawker Hurricane Mk I, V7780 of No.274 Squadron at Gerawala airfield near Tobruk in 1941
(©Imperial War Museum)

2in, a length of 53ft 9 1/2in and could reach a maximum speed of 273mph. The maximum internal bomb load was 2,200kg and it had a range of 1,421 miles. With a crew of five the type was powered by two 1,300hp inverted V-12 liquid-cooled Jumo 211 engines.

The Messerschmitt Bf 109F was the second generation of this iconic fighter and was powered with a 1,159hp inverted V-12 liquid-cooled DB 601N engine. It had a maximum speed of 382mph and was armed with a 20mm MG 151 cannon and two MG 17 machine-guns in the nose. At this time the Bf 109F was the best fighter over the desert.

The Fiat G.50 was the first modern monoplane fighter of the Regia Aeronautica making its maiden flight on the 26th February 1937. Powered by an 870hp Fiat A.74 air-cooled 14-cylinder radial engine it had a span of 36ft 0 3/4in, length of 26ft 3 1/3in, was equipped with a couple of 0.50in Breda-SAFAT machine-guns and had a maximum speed of 292mph.

Macchi MC.202 of 81a Squadriglia, 6° Gruppo somewhere in Libya
(©Italian Air Force)

A Messerschmitt Bf 110 of 9./ZG26 above the desert with two additional drop tanks under the wings
(©Italian Air Force)

The Curtiss Tomahawk first flew as the Hawk 81 in the United States on the 14th October 1938 and had a maximum speed of 357mph. With a span of 37ft 3 1/2in and a length of 31ft 8 9/16in it was equipped with four 0.303in machine guns in each wing and was powered by a 1,090hp liquid-cooled V-1710 Allison engine. Later the engine would be upgraded and the fuselage refined, thus becoming the Hawk 87, which the RAF called the Kittyhawk.

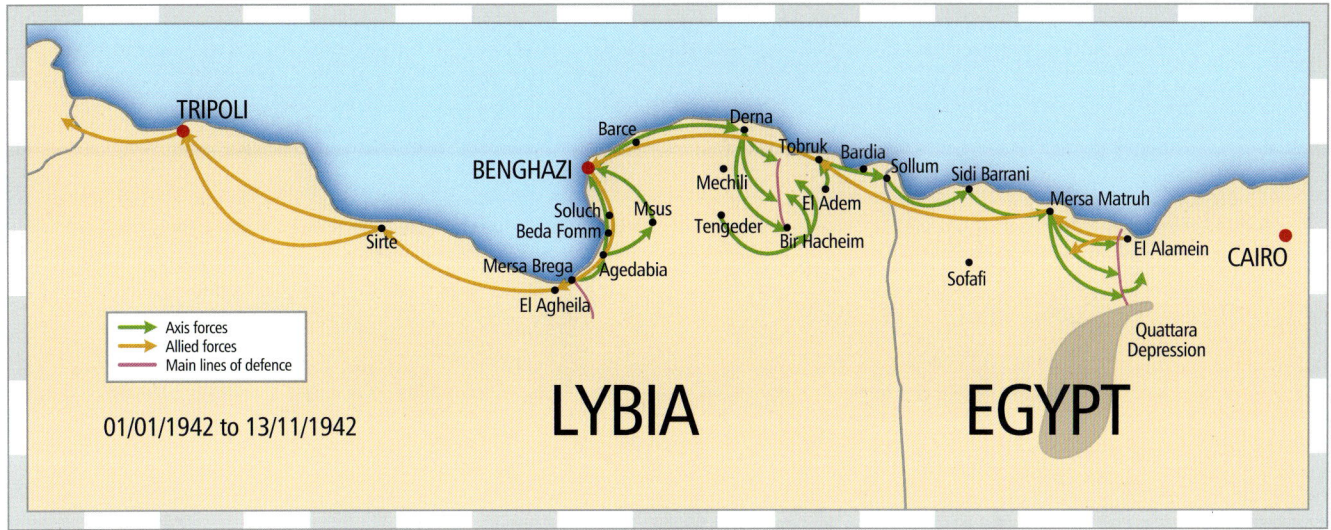

1942

'the end of the beginning'

When the Allied forces entrenched at El Agheila some 500 miles away from their previous bases they faced the same troubles that the Italian/German forces had done before, namely that the supply line was over-stretched. To prepare Operation Acrobat, the Tripolitania invasion, it was decided to withdraw from the front line in order to reduce the length of the supply lines and to make a base for the next move. However the DAK losses during Operation Crusader had been overestimated and on the 21st January 1942 the *Panzerarmee Afrika* launched Operation Theseus. In a couple of days the 2nd Armoured Brigade were defeated, thus enabling another Axis move westwards. By the 3rd February 1942, Benghazi and Timini fell into Axis hands and the Italian/German forces faced the entrenched Allied positions along the Gazala line of defence.

Battle of Gazala

Between February and May 1942, both sides used the time for replenishment as they were preparing for the next offensive. The *Panzerarmee Afrika* was the first to start the offensive with Operation Venice on the 26th May 1942. At the time the order of battle was as follows:

- **8th Army forces along the Gazala line of defence**
under command of Major-General Neil Ritchie:
  - Lieutenant-General William Henry Ewart Gott's XIII Corps with the 1st South African Infantry Division (1st, 2nd and 3rd South African Infantry Brigades), the 2nd South African Infantry Division (4th and 6th South African Infantry Brigades, 9th and 11th Indian Infantry Brigades), the 50th British Infantry Division (69th, 150th and 151st British Infantry Brigades) and the 1st and 32nd Army Tank Brigades.
  - Major-General Charles Willoughby Norrie's XXX Corps with the 1st British Armoured Division (2nd and 22nd British Armoured Brigades, 201st Guards Motor Brigade) and the 7th British Armoured Division (4th British Armoured Brigade, 7th British Motor Brigade, 3rd Indian Motor Brigade, 29th Indian Infantry Brigade and 1st Free French Brigade).

General Feldmarschall Erwin Rommel in discussion with Italian armoured troops. In the foreground is an Italian Semovente 75/18 tank
(©German Federal Archives)

  - Army reserve of the 5th Indian Infantry Division (10th Indian Infantry Brigade and 2nd Free French Brigade), the 10th Indian Infantry Division (20th, 21st and 25th Indian Infantry Brigades), the 11th Indian Infantry Brigade, the 1st British Armoured Brigade and the 5th Indian Infantry Brigade.

- **Panzerarmee Afrika under the command of General Erwin Rommel:**
  - *Generalleutnant* W. Nehring's *Deutches Afrika Korps* with the 15th and 21st Panzer Divisions and 90th *Leuchte* Division
  - *Generale di Corpo d'Armata* Ettore Baldassare's Italian XX Corpo with 132nd Armoured Division 'Ariete' and 101st Motorised Division 'Trieste'

- **Gruppe Crüwell under the command of General Ludwig Crüwell:**
  - *Generale di Corpo d'Armata* Benvenuto Gioda's Italian X Corpo with the 27th Infantry Division 'Brescia' and the 17th Infantry Division 'Pavia'
  - *Generale di Corpo d'Armata* Enea Navarini's Italian XXI Corpo with the 60th Infantry Division 'Sabratha' and the 102nd Motorized Division 'Trento'
  - 15th German *Shützen* Brigade

At 2.00pm on the 26th May the Italian X and XXI Corps launched a frontal attack against the Gazala line and the DAK moved in that direction to let the British believe it was the main thrust of the assault. However during the night the DAK forces moved southwards in order to turn against the Gazala line at the most southern point of Bir Hakeim. The 7th British Armoured

A Junkers Ju 88, somewhere Tunisia in 1942
(©German Federal Archives)

The crew of Douglas Boston Mk III W8376 of No.24 Squadron, South African Air Force, walk in after another sortie above enemy lines
(©Imperial War Museum)

Division strike against the DAK and the German had to take up a defensive position as the Bir Hakeim stronghold had not been taken after three days of tank battles. The southern end of the Gazala line was manned by the 1st Free French Brigade under the command of Général de Brigade Marie-Pierre Koenig and they fought well from the very first day of the Italian/German assault on the 26th May. By the 27th their position was surrounded and they had to fight elements of the Italian 132nd Armoured Division '*Ariete*'. From the 1st June the positions still held by Free French troops was attacked by elements of 90th *Leuchte* Division and 101st Motorised Division '*Trieste*'. The fighting lasted until the 11th June when 90th *Leuchte* Division overran the position. However during the previous night 2,700 troops of the 3,200 strong garrison escaped and reached the British lines of the 7th Motor Brigade.

At the same time the battle raged in the centre of the Gazala line in a place later called the 'Cauldron' where the *Ariete* and *Trieste* Divisions met up with the DAK forces after the encircling manoeuvre around Bir Hakeim. A counter-attack made by 1st British Armoured Division largely supported by the Desert Air Force did not reduce the Italian/German positions, but the Free French resistance at Bir Hakeim had elongated the Axis supply routes to the south of the Gazala line and given the British forces time to reorganize after the loss of the 'Cauldron'. The 21st Panzer Division reached El Adem on the 13th June and at that time after two weeks of fierce fighting 75% of the British tanks had been lost. On the 14st June General Auchinleck authorized the retreat from the Gazala line and on the 21st June the 2nd South African Infantry Division in Tobruk with 35,000 soldiers surrendered to *Generale di Corpo d'Armata* Enea Navarini.

Unloading a Messerschmitt Me 323D-1 Gigant in Tunisia in December 1942
(©German Federal Archives)

Battle of Mersa Matruh

After the defeat of the 8th Army on the Gazala line the Allied forces retreated into Egypt up to the fortress of Mersa Matruh on the shore. In this position Lieutenant-General William George Holmes' X Corps was created with two Infantry Divisions and Major-General Charles Willoughby Moke Norrie's XXX Corps prepared another strong line of defence around the village of El Alamein further east on the road to Cairo. Lieutenant-General William Henry Ewart Gott's XIII Corps completed the defensive layout south of Mersa Matruh. A great asset for the Allies was that the Desert Air Force ruled the sky above the front line. However Rommel hoped to destroy the Allied Infantry Divisions on the ground so launched a new offensive on the 26th June and three days later the XIII Corps had to retreat once more. The sacrifice of the X Corps made this retreat to El Alamein possible and thus this last line of defence became stronger with the addition of XIII Corps troops.

First battle of El Alamein

By the 30th June all Allied forces had withdrawn behind the El Alamein position, which over 30 miles went from the shore, to the north of the Quattara Depression. At the time Rommel was eager to crush the British forces and run to Cairo but after more than one month of fierce fighting in the desert the armoured divisions of the DAK and the Italian XX Corpo had suffered high attrition rates. Moreover the supply lines were once again over-stretched and the Desert Air Force and RAF units based on Malta took a heavy toll of them. As usual Rommel started the assault on the El Alamein positions even before getting replenishment for all his divisions. On the 1st July the DAK positioned along the coastline and the Italian XX Corpo on the right side headed for the well prepared positions of the 8th Army (XIII and XXX Corps). After three days of fighting the British positions remained and the Italian/German forces had to dig in in the face of continual air strikes by the bombers of the Desert Air Force.

At the time new bombers were in use, such as the Martin Baltimore, a twin-engined bomber that first flew on the 14th June 1941 having evolved from the Maryland. With a wingspan 61ft 4in and a length of 48ft 6in in the Mk V variant the Baltimore had a top speed of 305mph and could deliver up to 2,000lb of bombs over a maximum range of 980 miles. Also from the American aircraft industry came another medium bomber in the shape of Douglas Boston. The twin-engined design first flew on the 23rd December 1939 and had a wingspan of 61ft 4in and a length of 47ft 11 7/8in. Its maximum speed was 317mph and it could carry a maximum bomb load of 4,000lb for a range up to 945 miles. The Desert Air Force could also rely on the new medium bomber of the US Army Air Force, the North American B-25 Mitchell, which first flew on the 19th December 1940. It was powered by two 1,700hp Wright R-2600 radial engines, had a maximum speed of 272mph and could carry up to 2,000lb of bombs. With a wingspan of 67ft 7in and a length of 52ft 11in it had a maximum range of 1,350 miles.

Martin Baltimore FW605 in flight above the desert (©San Diego Air and Space Museum)

A Royal Air Force Martin Baltimore Mk IV bomber (©USAAF)

On the Axis side the Junkers Ju 88 twin-engined bomber was the main strike aircraft over the front. This aircraft first flew on the 21st December 1936 and had a wingspan of 65ft 10 1/2in and a length of 47ft 2 7/8in. It could fly at speeds up to 317mph for a maximum range of 1,429 miles and deliver had a combined bomb load of 1,500kg carried internally and/or externally.

On 8th July Lieutenant-General Ramsden, the new commander of the British XXX Corps, launched a counter-attack in the direction of Tel El Eisa on the coastline road but by the 12th July this had failed to push the German positions significantly. Another battle of attrition took place from the 14th July when the 2nd New Zealand Division attacked the *Brescia* and *Pavia* Divisions for the first time on Ruweisat Ridge. Even when the 90th *Leichte* and *Ariete* Divisions came to relieve the Italian infantry after three days of fighting the Allies took more than 2,000 Axis prisoners and nearly entirely destroyed three Italian divisions. After regrouping their forces the Allies attacked Ruweisat Ridge once again, then on to Tel El Eisa on the 21st July but they did not succeed in going through the Axis lines. Even if the first battle of El Alalmein was not really an Allied victory the aim was achieved in that it stopped the Axis forces in their advance towards Alexandria and gave time to prepare the next move. The price was high though as the Allies had suffered 13,000 casualties. In early August 1942, Sir Winston Churchill decided to replace General Auchinleck with General Harold Alexander and gave 8th Army command to the then XIII Corps commander, Lieutenant-General William Henry Ewart Gott. Sadly Lieutenant-General Gott was killed when his transport aircraft was shot down during the flight to take up his command and so it was Lieutenant-General Bernard Montgomery who took command of the 8th Army on the 13th August 1942.

Battle of Alam el Halfa

After the first battles around the El Alamein fortified positions both forces were exhausted and so they had to replenish before starting another round. For the Axis troops the supply chain was a great distance away because Tobruk and Benghazi were respectively 400 and 800 miles from the front line. As already noted the Desert Air Force kept the upper hand in the skies above the battlefield even if the *Jagdgeschwadern* could still take their toll of the Allied aircraft. The Allied supply lines were even longer as the equipment had to travel by sea from Britain and the United States and the sea lanes of the Atlantic Ocean lanes were less than secure in 1942.

The Axis forces started their new offensive on the night of the 30th August by skirting on the south the stronger Allied positions, but from the start things went wrong because the RAF spotted the concentration of vehicles gathering near the front line and the Desert Air Force undertook a series of bombing raids against the Axis forces. As General Montgomery considered that the 8th Army was not well prepared for a new offensive the orders were to resist and rely on the Air Force to blunt the Italian/German offensive. He was correct in his thinking and for the first time the tank losses were roughly the same when the Axis units retreated to their initial starting positions on the 2nd September 1942. Lieutenant-General Brian Horrocks' forces had weathered the assault and the 8th Army could therefore continue its build-up behind the El Alamein positions. This was to be the last significant offensive in the Western Desert by Rommel.

Second Battle of El Alamein

For the next round the Allied Forces were getting stronger every day and General Bernard Montgomery's 8th Army was organized as follows:

- Lieutenant-General Herbert Lumsden's X Corps with the 1st British Armoured Division (2nd British Armoured Brigade, 7th British Motorized Brigade and 'Hammerforce' from 8th Armoured Division), the 8th British Armoured Division (24th British Armoured Brigade and 'Hammerforce' from 1st Armoured Division) and Divisional troops
- Lieutenant-General Brian Horrocks' XIII Corps with the 7th British Armoured Division (4th British Light Armoured Brigade, 22nd British Armoured Brigade and 1st Free French Brigade), the 44th British Division (131st, 132nd and 133rd Brigades) and the 50th British Division (69th and 101st British Infantry Brigades, 1st Greek Brigade and 2nd Free French Brigade)
- Lieutenant-General Sir Oliver Leese's XIII Corps with the 4th Indian Infantry Division (5th, 7th and 161st Indian Infantry Divisions), the 9th Australian Infantry Division (20th, 24th and 26th Australian Infantry Brigades), the 2nd New Zealand Division (5th and 6th New Zealand Infantry Brigades and 9th British Armoured Brigade), the 1st South African Infantry Division (1st, 2nd and 3rd South African Infantry Brigades) and the 51st (Highland) Division (152nd, 153rd and 154th Infantry Brigades).

On the other side for the last great battle of the Western Desert, the Italian forces were as follows:
- *Generale* Enrico Fratini's X Corpo with the 17th Infantry Division '*Pavia*', the 185th Parachutist Division '*Folgore*' and the 27th Infantry Division '*Brescia*'
- *Generale* Giusepe de Stefanis' XX Corpo with the 132nd Armoured Division '*Ariete*', the 101st Motorised Division '*Trieste*' and the 133rd Armoured Division '*Littorio*'
- *Generale* Allesandro Gloria's XXI Corpo with the 25th Infantry Division '*Bologna*' and the 102nd Motorized Division '*Trento*'

And the German forces had gathered as follows on the front line:
- Under *General* Georg Stumme's direct command: the 90th and 164th *Leichte* Divisions and the *Ramcke Falschirmjäger* Brigade
- *Generalleutnant* Wilhelm Ritter von Thoma's *Deutches Afrika Korps* with the 15th and 21st Panzer Divisions

At the time the Western Desert Air Force had strengthened in numbers and quality as well. They could now boast up to fifty-five British, one Greek, twelve USAAF and ten Commonwealth squadrons of combat aircraft comprising 605 fighters, 254 light and medium bombers and 61 heavy bombers. The Italian/German Air Forces had a strength of 247 fighters, 72 dive bombers and 171 medium bombers. So, on the 23rd October 1942, General Bernard Montgomery was ready to launch the new offensive against the Italian/German positions. At 9.40pm a formidable Allied artillery (creeping) barrage started pounding the enemy positions with up to 1,000 guns, something that had not been seen on the front line since WWI. Twenty minutes later the four infantry divisions of XXX Corps began to move in the direction of the strongest point of the front line. The aim was to create a passage for the Armoured Brigades of X Corps. On the southern sector of the front a secondary attack was undertaken by the 7th Armoured Division. On the 25th the two arms of the attack had achieved no concrete results with a mere 5 miles advance inside the Italian/German line of defence, even with continual bombing by the Western Desert Air Force. On the 26th the counter-attack came from the Panzer Divisions as *Generalfeldmarschall* Erwin Rommel came back from sick leave, quickly evaluated the situation and ordered a push on the northern part of the front. For the next six days a series of attacks were undertaken by both sides, but the situation did not clearly evolve. Operation Supercharge was launched on the 2nd November with a seven-hour aerial bombardment and a four and a half hour artillery barrage in front of the 2nd New Zealand Division's line of progress. They were followed by the tanks of the

Italian General Ugo Cavallero and Ettore Batisco in discussion in front of a Savoia-Marchetti S.79 in Lybia on the 17th March 1942
(©Italian Air Force)

An SdKfz 251 in a Wehrmacht communication centre in the desert on the 1st June 1942
(©German Federal Archives)

1st Armoured Division, but General Montgomery had to add the tanks of the 7th Armoured Division and four infantry brigades into the battle to get some results during the night of the 2nd November. It was only on the 4th November that the attack got significant results when both amoured divisions succeeded in breaking the defences between the German and Italian positions. The British tanks started to circle the Panzer divisions by running towards the shore. Due to a lack of fuel for the British tanks and a fast retreat from the DAK forces they escaped the trap before it closed. It was not the case however for many Italian divisions, which did not have enough lorries for their soldiers, so they had to walk westwards. The Italian/German rout started on the 6th November and Rommel decided to mount a delaying action around Sidi Barani in order to give time for the other units to escape from the El Alamein area, but this action did not succeed and the Egyptian territory was cleared of Axis troops by the 11th November. After the battle the British Prime Sir Winston Churchill said on the radio "Now this is not the end. It is not even the beginning of the end. But it is, perhaps, the end of the beginning."

Battle of El Agheila

The last battle in the Western Desert between the Italian and German forces and the British 8th Army was fought near El Agheila, the starting point of the deployment of the *Deutches Afrika Korps* some 18 months earlier. But in December 1942 the *Panzerarmee* represented only a small part of what it used to be. The men were exhausted and because since the 8th November another front had been opened in Tunisia and this had been given top priority from the *Oberkommando der Wehrmacht*, the *Panzerarmee Afrika* did not received many supplies. Moreover the fleeing German and Italian soldiers had to cope with constant harassment from the Desert Air Force, which by then had acquired complete air superiority in the region. The first elements of the British 8th Army entered Benghazi, the capital city of Cyrenaica, on the 22nd November and were in front of the El Agheila defensive line a week later. The battle started on the 11th December with an encircling manoeuvre and by the 15th the battle was over. The Italian/German forces had to flee once again, with the last rearguard action taking place 100 miles west of El Agheila on the 18th December 1942. A small interception action was organised around the port of Buerat by the Germans but Montgomery attacked and reduced it on 15th December, and the last elements of the *Panzerarmee Afrika* left Tripoli on the 19th December after destroying the harbour. The 8th Army entered Tripoli on the 22nd January 1943 and at the same time the Germans had retreated behind an old French line of defence in Tunisia some 200 miles westwards, called the Mareth Line.

Grumman Martlet and Supermarine Seafire about to take off from HMS Formidable's flight deck in November 1942
(©Imperial War Museum)

1943

Operation Torch

To initiate another front on the African Continent and increase the pressure on the Axis forces the US and the British prepared an invasion of French North Africa territory and for that purpose organised secret negotiations with local Vichy authorities like Admiral Darland and with local resistance movements. From the beginning the main places to land were selected as being along the shores near Casablanca, Oran and Algiers. Tunis was a very important objective too as it cut the supply route to the remnants of the *Panzerarmee Afrika* but was too close to Axis airfields in Sicily and Sardinia, thus the landings there would have been too dangerous. Finally the landings were organised as follows:
- British Lieutenant-General Kenneth Anderson's Eastern Task Force to land on Algiers, Bougie, Djidjelli and Bône in French Algeria with the

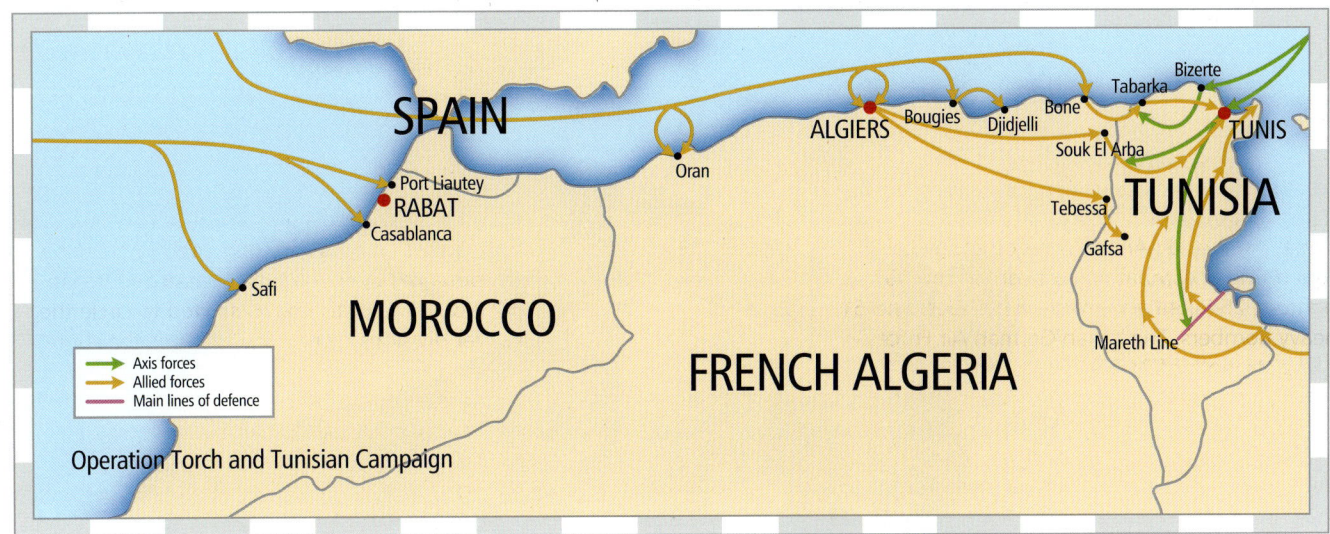

A Grumman Martlet Mk II of No.888 Naval Air Squadron, HMS Formidable at Oran airfield in December 1942 (©USN)

A wrecked Messerschmitt Bf 110E of 9./ZG26 at Fuka airfield, Egypt on the 13th November 1942 (©Australian War Memorial)

American troops aboard a landing craft about to land on Oran beaches during Operation Torch in November 1942 (©Imperial War Museum)

Fairey Albacore Mk I of No.820 Naval Air Squadron, HMS Formidable during Operation Torch in November 1942 (©Imperial War Museum)

A Supermarine Seafire Mk IIc of No.885 Naval Air Squadron on the flight deck of HMS Formidable in the Mediterranean in December 1942 (©Imperial War Museum)

78th British Infantry Division, Nos.1 & 6 Commandos and the 34th US Infantry Division; a total of 20,000 troops
- US Major-General Lloyd Fredendall's Centre Task Force to land on Oran in French Algeria with the 1st US Infantry Division, the 1st US Armoured Division, the 1st US Ranger Battalion, the 3rd/6th US Armoured Infantry Regiment and the US Parachute Task Force; a total of 18,500 troops
- US Major-General George S. Patton's Western Task Force to land on Safi, Casablanca and Port-Liautey in French Morocco with three sub-task forces from the 3rd US Infantry Division, the 9th US Infantry Division and the 2nd US Armoured Division; a total of 35,000 troops

These tasks forces were supported by three naval air groups on HMS Argus (No.880 Naval Air Squadron), HMS Avenger (Nos.802 & 883 Naval Air Squadrons), HMS Furious (Nos.801, 807 & 822 Naval Air Squadrons), HMS Biter (No.800 Naval Air Squadron), HMS Dasher (Nos.804 & 891 Naval Air Squadrons), USS Ranger (VT-41, VF-41 & VF-9), USS Sawanee (VT-27, VF-27, VF-28 & VF-30), USS Sangamon (VT-26) and USS Chenango (USAAF 33rd Fighter Group) and Force H around the two aircraft-carriers HMS Victorious (Nos.885, 888, 893 & 820 Naval Air Squadrons) and HMS Formidable (Nos.809, 882, 884, 817 & 832 Naval Air Squadrons).

On the other side the French military forces were organized with 60,000 troops in Morocco, 50,000 in Algeria and 15,000 in Tunisia. These were equipped with coastal artillery, 210 out-of-date tanks and 500 aircraft.

The landings started on the 8th November 1942 but the French forces were for the most part loyal to the Vichy government, so did not welcome the invasion. In Morocco at Safi, the coastal batteries opened fire against the invasion

force but the garrison surrendered in the afternoon of the 8th November and the last defenders two days later. At Port-Liautey the objectives were reached under fire from French artillery positions. At Casablanca there was a naval battle between the task force and the capital ship *Jean Bart* which was finally disabled on the 10th November by 16in calibre US naval gunfire. At Oran, French batteries and the Centre Task Force

A PzKpfw VI Tiger heavy tank of Schwere Panzer Abteilung 504 in Tunisia in 1943
(©German Federal Archives)

Hurricane Mk IIDs of No.6 Squadron taking off from an airfield at Gabès in Tunisia on the 6th April 1943
(©Imperial War Museum)

A Supermarine Spitfire Mk Vb of No.152 Squadron on a PSP area at Tingley, Algeria
(©Imperial War Museum)

A Supermarine Spitfire Mk Ic of No.1 Squadron, South African Air Force in 1943
(©South African Air Force)

invasion fleet exchanged fire until the garrison surrendered on the 9th November. At Algiers, on the 8th November, the landings on five beaches either side of the town enabled the British forces to quickly surround the French garrison and at 8.00pm they surrendered. Actually in three days of fighting the French forces suffered 3,343 casualties and the Allies 2,661 casualties. It cannot be said that the landings were 'easy' because the Allied casualties represented 30% of those who would fall during the Normandy landings on the 6th June 1944.

The Axis reaction

Even if the Axis headquarters did not guess that the invasion force was to land on the Moroccan and Algerian coasts they were swift to react to the new situation. Due to the lack of determined resistance against the Allied Invasion Force, the Germans immediately started Operation Anton, the occupation of Vichy France territory. They raced to Toulon harbour in order to seize the French Navy's highly valuable assets. With this in mind on the evening of the 10th November the German 1. Army advanced from south-west France to Toulon and German 7th Army moved along the Rhône Valley to Vichy and Toulon. On the 11th November the German forces reached the Mediterranean. Under threat from the German troops the French Naval Authorities negotiated to gain time and prepare the scuttling of the ships in the harbour, which was finally done on the 27th November 1942. Amid the scuttled ships were the battleships *Strasbourg*, *Dunkerque* and *Provence*, *Commandant Teste* seaplane tender, the heavy cruiser *Dupleix*, *Foch*, *Algérie* & *Colbert* and light cruisers *Marseillaise*, *Jean de Vienne* and *La Galissonière*.

The race for Tunis

The second part of the Axis reaction was to invade Tunisia and on the 9th November General von Arnim's German 5th Army started landing around Bizerte and Tunis harbours. To counter this action the Eastern Task Force, renamed British 1st Army, started moving eastwards from their Algiers landing zones and the first new landings were organised on the port of Bougies and Bône on the 11th & 12th November. The plan was to follow the two roads going from Algiers to Bizerte and Tunis, when after 30 miles they entrenched in order to wait for the build-up of their forces. It was very much the same situation for the Axis units. By the 22nd December, the Allies had 54,000 British, 78,000 American and 7,000 French troops. At this time the French Army resumed its action against the Axis forces but was poorly equipped and trained in comparison to their British and American allies. After five days of hard fighting the Allies had to return to their original positions and they suffered 20,743 casualties.

Battle of Kasserine Pass

The German forces, still under the command of *Feldmarschall* Erwin Rommel, were the first to move when the 21st Panzer Division attacked the American positions around the Kasserine Pass in the Atlas Mountains to the west of Tunisia on the 19th February 1943. This was the first major engagement of American troops and they were pushed back over 50 miles, however from the 20th November they were reinforced with British troops and succeeded in stopping the German advance. The 8th Army also arrived near the Mareth Line in south Tunisia, where they represented a danger to the Axis forces, so the German offensive on the Kasserine Pass was halted. During that period the Allied forces suffered 10,000 casualties and lost 183 tanks while the Axis had 2,000 casualties and lost 34 tanks.

A British Churchill Tank and other vehicles parade in Tunis on the 8th May 1943
(©Imperial War Museum)

Douglas Boston Mk III, AL683 of No.24 Squadron, South African Air Force at Zuara, Tripolitania in 1943
(©Imperial War Museum)

Flight Lieutenant W.H. Pentland of No.417 Squadron, Royal Canadian Air Force, waiting to start up his Supermarine Spitfire Mk Vc BR195 at Goubrine airfield, Tunisia in May 1943
(©Imperial War Museum)

A Grant tank of the 1st US Armoured Division in Tunisia during the battle of Kasserine Pass
(©U.S. Army)

Battle of the Mareth Line

On the 6th March the Axis forces had once again gained the initiative when they started advancing towards the town of Medenine in southern Tunisia from their positions on the Mareth Line. This action actually was a defensive one in order to delay the British offensive on the Mareth Line and the Axis troops retreated that same evening. On the 19th March, XXX Corps started advancing against the Mareth line and the 50th British Infantry Division managed to push the Italian lines near Zarat, but on the 22nd a counter-offensive made by 15th Panzer Division pushed back the British. On the night of the 23rd/24th another attack against the line was launched by the 4th Indian Infantry Division. In the meantime, General Montgomery had formed the New Zealand Corps (a purpose built Corps), which turned round the Matmata Hills and thus could strike at the back of the Mareth Line via the Tebaga Gap. The attack started on the 21st March but was slow to advance against the 164th *Leichtes Afrika* Division and the 21st Panzer Division. It was the same for the XXX Corps, so when the 1st British Armoured Division added its punch to the New Zealand Corps there was a breakthrough inside the German positions and by the 28th March all the Axis forces retreated to the north to avoid being overrun. On the 31st March 1943, Gabès was liberated.

A damaged Focke-Wulf Fw 190A-4 of III./SKG10 at Tunis El Aouina airfield in May 1943 (©Library of U.S. Congress)

US soldiers walking along the Kasserine Pass, Tunisia in February 1943 (©U.S. Army)

Supermarine Spitfire Mk Vs assembled by the Special Erection Party for Operation Torch, being serviced on Gibraltar (©Imperial War Museum)

Two Supermarine Spitfire Mk Vbs of No.40 Squadron, South African Air Force above the Tunisian coast in 1943 (©Imperial War Museum)

Douglas Boston Mk III, Z2205 of No.114 Squadron at Canrobert, French Algeria in 1943 (©Imperial War Museum)

Macchi MC.202s of 168a Squadriglia in 1943 (©Italian Air Force)

Squadron Leader M. Rook, commanding officer of No.43 Squadron in front of Supermarine Spitfire Mk Vc, JK101, FT•Z at Jemappes, Algeria. He was qualified at the time as the tallest pilot in the RAF (©Imperial War Museum)

Battle of El Guettar

Simultaneously with the Mareth Line assault the American troops left their positions above the Kasserine Pass in order to invade the valleys below, and particularly the little town of El Guettar which had a direct road to Gabès. The 1st and 9th U.S. Divisions fought well and settled in the south of El Gettar on the 23rd March.

Battle of Wadi Akarit

This battle was initiated by the Allies in the southern front to push back the Axis forces from the region west of Sfax. It started on the 6th April 1943 and after a failed counter-attack by the 1st Italian Army the Axis troops had to retreat again on the 7th April. The same day the American troops of II Corps met the soldiers of the British 8th Army on the road between El Guettar and Gabès. The pursuit continued northwards for 140 miles and the towns of Sfax and Sousse were liberated. The Axis forces thereafter entrenched in defensive positions 25 miles south of Cap Bon.

The last battle in Africa

For the last battle the Allied forces were reorganized as follows:
- Lieutenant-General Kenneth Anderson's British First Army from the north coast including Lieutenant-General Charles Allfrey's British V Corps, Lieutenant-General John Crocker's British IX Corps, Lieutenant-General Marie-Louise Koëltz' French XIX Corps and Major-General Omar Bradley's US II Corps
- General Bernard Mongomery's British 8th Army from the south with Lieutenant-General Sir Oliver Leese's British XXX Corps, Lieutenant-General Miles Dempsey's XIII Corps and Lieutenant-General Bernard Freyberg's British X Corps

On the morning of the 22nd April 1943, the 46th British Infantry Division launched its offensive against the Axis positions and thus led the way for the British 6th and 1st Armoured Divisions. The British V Corps and the American II Corps started their offensive the next day along the northern coastline of Tunisia. As it was evident that the terrain in front of the British 8th Army was too difficult for an offensive General Alexander, the Commander-in-Chief of this Theatre of Operation, decided to transfer the 7th British Armoured Division, the 4th Indian Infantry Division and the 201st Guards Motor Brigade to the British 1st Army in the north to help them break through there. The new attack was launched on the 5th May, by the 7th May Tunis was liberated by British forces and Bizerte by the US II Corps.

The last Axis resistance in North Africa ceased on the 11th May 1943, when 22,000 Germans surrendered to the Free French Forces in the mountainous Zaghouan sector. With 100,000

A Lockheed Hudson Mk VI of No.216 Squadron above the Tunisian battlefront in 1943 (©Imperial War Museum)

German and 200,000 Italian soldiers taken prisoner at the end of the Tunisian campaign, the OKB estimated that this was a stronger blow than the loss of Stalingrad a few months earlier. This time it was the beginning of the end.

Crusader tanks at El Hamma, Tunisia on the 29th March 1943 (©Imperial War Museum)

Colour Reference

With so many colours and so many paint manufacturers nowadays, we thought that you might like the following cross-reference chart for the major shades relating to the air war over the Western Desert.

Acrylics

🎯 RAF

	Akan	GS Mr Aqueous	Humbrol	Lifecolor	MM	Tamiya	Xtracrylix
Dark Green BS241	-	H330	A163	UA091	077	XF-80	XA1001
Dark Earth	70010	H72	A29	UA092	078	XF-52*	XA1002
Medium Sea Grey BS637	70016	H335	A165	UA094	094	XF-83	XA1003
Middle Stone	-	H71	A225	UA097	076	-	XA1009
Azure Blue	70004	-	A157	UA098	092	-	XA1026
Interior Grey-Green	70007	-	-	079	-	XA1010	

★ USAAF

	Akan	GS Mr Aqueous	Humbrol	Lifecolor	MM	Tamiya	Xtracrylix
Olive Drab ANA 613	72033	H52	A66	UA005	091	XF-62	XA1112
Neutral Grey	72038*	H53	-	UA046	-	XF-53	XA1133
Zinc Chromate Green	72004	-	-	-	059	-	-
Yellow Zinc Chromate Primer	-	-	-	UA134	067	-	-

✠ Luftwaffe

	Akan	GS Mr Aqueous	Humbrol	Lifecolor	MM	Tamiya	Xtracrylix
RLM 02 Grau	71045	H70	A240	UA071	056	XF-22	XA1201
RLM 04 Gelb	71046	H413	-	UA140	090	-	XA1213
RLM 27 Gelb	-	-	-	-	-	-	-
RLM 65 Hellblau	71054	H67	A65	UA061	-	XF-23	XA1202
RLM 70 Schwarzgrün	71056	H65	A241	UA051	088	XF-13*	XA1204
RLM 71 Dunkelgrün	71057	H64	A242	UA052	087	XF-61	XA1205
RLM 78 Hellblau	71063	H418	A248	UA062	-	-	XA1214
RLM 79 Sandgelb	71064	H66	A249	UA081	-	-	XA1209
RLM 80 Grun	71065	H420	-	UA506	-	-	XA1215

🇮🇹 Regia Aeronautica

	Akan	GS Mr Aqueous	Humbrol	Lifecolor	MM	Tamiya	Xtracrylix
Verde Anticorrosione	-	-	-	UA116	-	-	-
Grigio Azzurro Chiaro	-	-	-	UA113	-	-	-
Nocciola Chiaro 4	-	-	-	UA112	-	-	-
Verde Oliva Scuro 2	-	-	-	UA111	-	-	-

Enamels

🎯 RAF

	Humbrol	Revell	White Ensign	Xtracolor
Dark Green BS241	163	-	ACRN09	X1
Dark Earth	29	82	ACRN10	X2
Medium Sea Grey BS637	165	-	ACRN04	X3
Middle Stone	225	-	ACRN11	-
Azure Blue	157	-	ACRN12	-
Interior Grey-Green	78	-	ACRN20	X10

★ USAAF

	Humbrol	Revell	White Ensign	Xtracolor
Olive Drab ANA 613	66	-	ACUS12	X112
Neutral Grey	-	374	ACUS13	X133
Yellow Zinc Chromate Primer	-	-	ACUS23	X408

✠ Luftwaffe

	Humbrol	Revell	White Ensign	Xtracolor
RLM 02 Grau	240	362	ACLW12	X201 + X409
RLM 04 Gelb	-	-	ACLW21	X213
RLM 27 Gelb	-	-	-	-
RLM 65 Hellblau	65	-	ACLW03	X202
RLM 70 Schwarzgrün	241	46	ACLW02	X204
RLM 71 Dunkelgrün	242	68	ACLW11	X205
RLM 78 Hellblau	248	-	ACLW17	X214
RLM 79 Sandgelb	249	-	ACLW18	X209
RLM 80 Grun	-	-	ACLW19	X215

🇮🇹 Regia Aeronautica

	Humbrol	Revell	White Ensign	Xtracolor
Verde Anticorrosione	-	-	-	-
Grigio Azzurro Chiaro	-	-	ACRA15	-
Nocciola Chiaro	-	-	ACRA10	-
Verde Oliva Scuro 2	-	-	ACRA09	-

* Approximation

Note 1 – Lifecolors are all matched to the Federal Standard, not the British Standard, so they are approximations for British colours

Note 1 – All Humbrol paints, be they acrylic or enamel, are identified with the same numbering system, however for clarity here we have prefixed all acrylics with 'A'

MM = Mission Models Hobby Paints

Junkers Ju 52/3m

1/144th

by Steve A. Evans

With the Ju 52 being such a well-known and well-used machine, it would be criminal not to tell its story in miniature. The Eduard 1/144th scale kits are all beautiful and fill a little niche that many modellers dip into now and then, just for something different. This aircraft is available in every other major scale but its sheer size will be a restriction for some modellers. Eduard give us a very nice rendition of the Junkers transport, available in two kits, one military and one civil. This being the military version you get four versions in the box, all with very nice markings. The little cardboard package contains three sprues of dark grey-coloured plastic and one clear, a small instruction book of 12 pages and a single decal sheet. The plastic is well formed in the most part but there is a bit of flash here and there to deal with, and considering the size of some of the parts you have to be careful with the trimming. The four versions on offer are illustrated with lovely full-colour painting and marking guides and the decals themselves are beautifully printed, in perfect register with bright colours. It's going to be interesting to see how they react to the corrugated surfaces but they look nice on the sheet anyway.

Construction

There are only 55 parts in total in this box and some of them won't be used so you can imagine that the build part of it isn't going to take too long, especially as the interior is pretty basic. It consists of just three plastic parts, four transparent bits and a single decal for the instrument panel. There are no control columns, even though they are shown in the instructions and nothing at all in the main cabin. That's not really a problem because without the large loading

The box is tiny but a pleasure to behold with striking graphics and lovely art

Technical Data
Eduard 1/144th Junkers Ju 52/3m
Kit No.: 4424   Material: IM
Manufacturer: Eduard, Czech Republic
UK Price: £12.99

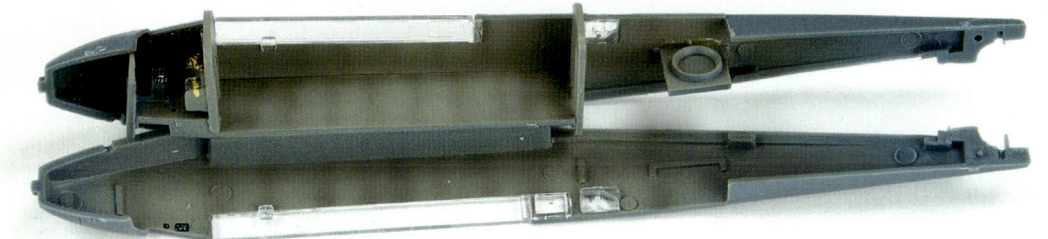

This is the standard kit interior. There are etched sets available from Eduard for both the military and civilian versions

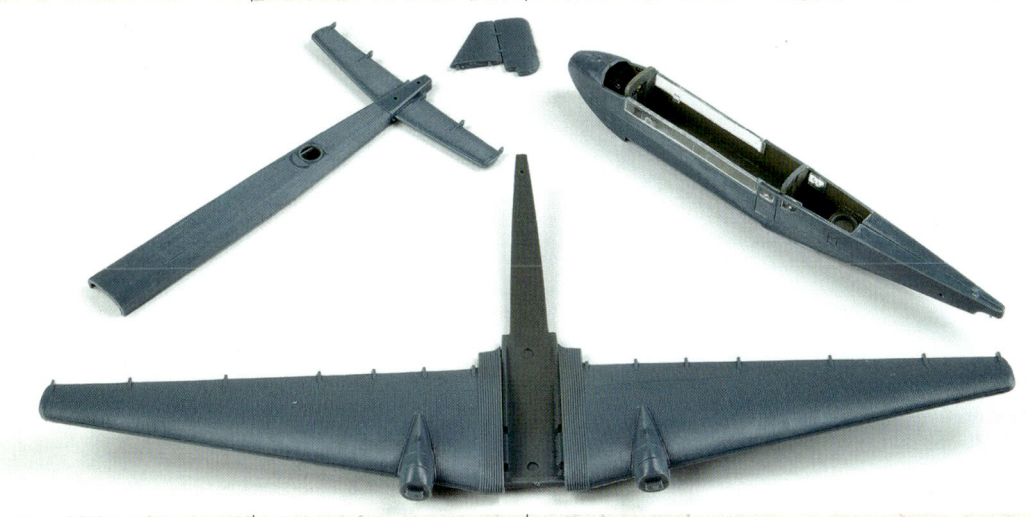

The main sections of the kit are neatly moulded and the fit isn't too bad. The corrugated skins are beautifully done, though

The wings need a little help to fit with plastic card filling the gaps at the wing roots but the separate wing and tail control sections look excellent

Note the plasticard at the wing root, the average fit of the clear bits but the very welcome pre-cut masks

RLM 04 Gelb sections first, this should make it look very Germanic

RLM 65 underside, the clean version at the moment

RLM 71 base coat with the masking for the hard-edged pattern. The Tamiya tape is used for the edging, filled in with any old rubbish

The RLM 70 is very dark but gives a nice contrast with the paler green, as the masking is applied for the additional RLM 02 areas

door on the right side open, you can't see in there anyway.

The fuselage is completed by the upper section which has the horizontal stabilizers moulded in situ and the clear canopy. There is a little wind-driven turbine generator on the right and the vertical tail will need to be fitted, although I did leave the little MG 15 machine gun off until later.

The wings are next and they are simple affairs as well. The moulded corrugations are neat and the fit is reasonable, although they are a bit 'gappy' at the wing roots. The separate control surfaces are very nice but they do need careful alignment with lots of trims and trial fits to get them into the right spot.

Completing the build are the undercarriage units and the engine nacelles. All are a little simplified but still look pretty good in this scale. The engines, once wrapped in their nacelles are lacking detail but it's not too noticeable, thankfully.

Colour & Markings

Eduard's decal choices in this box are inspired. Each of the four versions has something different and striking about the markings. There are two from the Med and North Africa, one from Crete and one from France. There are splashes of colour, squadron badges, lots of theatre markings and crazy paint jobs to go with them as well.

The instructions quote Gunze-Sangyo paints throughout the build and painting stages and with the right shades in my own store, I followed them to the letter. The version I chose, with the large areas of RLM 02 on the upper surface, is a bit of an enigma with some people claiming that it's actually a hybrid colour scheme using the pre-war colours of RLM 62/63 with the RLM 71. Anyway, I followed the instructions and after a bit of primer and lots of masking, the paint was applied. RLM 04 features heavily on this particular machine, which should brighten it up, with the RLM 02 applied over the standard RLM 70/71 splinter camouflage. I left this last part quite thin, so that the original camouflage shows through in a couple of places.

Weathering in this small scale has to be subtle, so other than a little paint chipping along the wing roots, especially on the right around the loading door, and some Tamiya Smoke, I kept it quite clean. I added a bit more exhaust staining on the underside using pastel dust and it was sealed in under a coat of Johnson's Klear for the decals.

Being such a tiny thing there are just 14 decals to apply for this version, with no stencils and just the national markings and individual aircraft badges and lettering. The decals worked really well, although they are prone to getting stuck if you try to move them about too much on the undulating surface. The trick is to slide them off the backing sheet as close to the final position as possible. With the help of Microscale setting and softening solutions they settled down really well, with just a couple of tiny bits of silvering to be dealt with before the final finish was applied.

Final Details

There are a few small bits to add at the end and annoyingly one of them is the D/F loop which isn't included in the kit, even though it is shown in the instructions and you're even told what colour to paint it! The pitot probe is also another addition that needs adding, with mine made from stretched sprue. If you decide to get the etched frets for this kit then those items are on there, along with masses of interior detail as well.

The final stages are applying the matt coat

Even in this scale there will be plenty of delicate bits at the end. Additional bits are the D/F loop aerial and the pitot probe

(Xtracolor XDFF of course) demasking the clear parts and fitting the aerial wire from tail to the mast above the cockpit and the MG 15 machine gun into position on the upper decking.

Verdict

The Ju 52 is one of those uniquely individual aircraft that just about everybody loves and this Eduard kit is a fine example of it. The detail is good, the general fit and finish is acceptable and the marking choices in the box are inspired. It's not perfect, with some missing parts, flash to deal with and some of the joints are a little clumsy. However, with a little care and attention you get a fine looking 'Tante Ju'. Go the extra mile with the etched frets available and it really does come to life, so this one is recommended to anyone who wants to do something a little different.

Colours Used

Gunze-Sangyo Mr Aqueous Color acrylic:	
H64 RLM 71	H65 RLM 70
H67 RLM 65	H70 RLM 02
H413 RLM 04	

References

- Die Junkers 52 am Zweiten Welthring Bildreport (Motorbuch Verlag 1991)
- Junkers Ju 52 – Aircraft & Legend by H.J. Nowarra (Haynes Publishing Group 1987 ISBN: 0-85429-592-5)
- Junkers Ju 52 by H.J. Nowarra (Schiffer ISBN: 0-88740-523-1)
- Junkers Ju 52, Luftwaffe Profile No.14 (Schiffer ISBN: 0-7643-0952-8)
- Junkers Ju 52 by M. Ryés, P. Skulski & J. Magnuszewski, Model Fan Encyclopedia No.4 (AJaKS 2001 ISBN: 83-914521-3-1)
- Ju 52 In Action No.186 by H-H Stapfer, H-J Mau & G. Punka (Squadron/Signal Publications 2003 ISBN: 0-89747-448-1)
- The Luftwaffe In Camera 1939-1942 by A. Price (Budding Books 2000
- Transporter Volume 1 & 2 by M. Pegg (Classic Publications 2007 ISBN: 1-903223-63-46 & 1-903223-64-4)

Historical Significance

It seems like a massive understatement to call this aircraft 'historically significant'. It was the backbone of the Luftwaffe transport fleet from the first day of the War, right up to the last. The 'Tante Ju' ('Auntie Ju') was used everywhere, all the time and for everything from hauling fuel to ferrying the wounded back to safety. Universally loved wherever it went, the crews had no choice but to fly it as no credible alternative was ever produced in any numbers. In North Africa, great swarms of them ranged over the desert and the Mediterranean Sea, desperately trying to resupply the troops below. With no provision for the heat of North Africa, flying the aircraft in the hot air was a tricky affair when it was fully loaded, and many of the rough runways used by the transport squadrons had to be extended for the longer take-off runs. Massive assembly areas had to be cleared as well to cope with the large numbers of aircraft at each supply base. It wasn't an easy task and with limited air cover, the Ju 52 crews paid a heavy price for getting the materiel of war to the front lines. With a top speed barely over 160mph the lumbering tri-motors were easy pickings for the Allied aircraft. Even medium bombers like the B-25 Mitchell and B-26 Marauder went hunting the flocks of Junkers and with some success too. It wasn't unusual to see 50 or 60 of these aircraft at a time making a run over the sea and sand and with very poor defensive armament the ungainly looking machines were hard pressed just to survive. But survive they did and even today, all these years later, there are still eight wartime Ju 52s flying. The oldest of these was built in 1936, once named 'Iron Annie' this aircraft is now operated by Lufthansa out of Hamburg in beautiful old style livery, proudly wearing the name 'Templehof'.

✠ **Messerschmitt Bf 110D-1, W/Nr.2354, 3U+DT, 9./ZG 26, Daba, North Africa**
RLM 79 upper surfaces with RLM 80 mottling; undersides in RLM 65. White fuselage band and undersides of wingtips; code in black with yellow 'D'. Spinner front in yellow, unit badge on nose

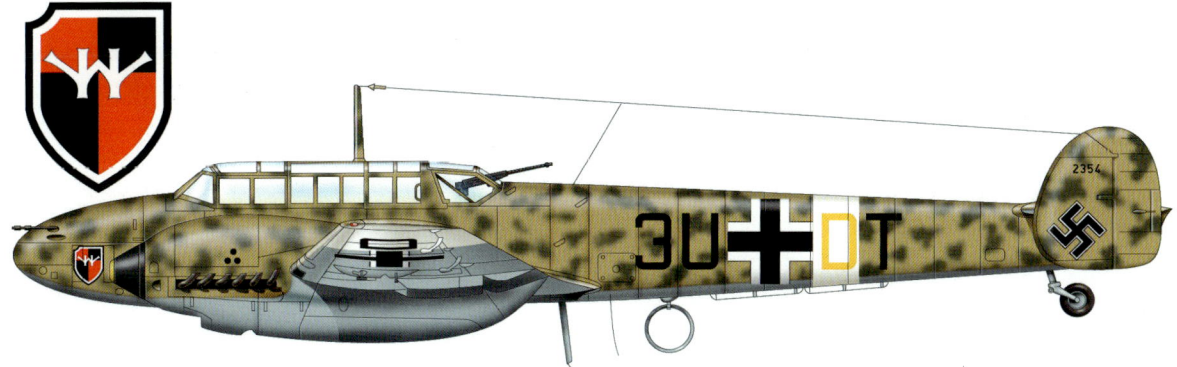

✠ **Messerschmitt Bf 110E-2, 3U+KT, 9./ZG 26, North Africa, March 1942**
RLM 78/79 scheme with RLM 27 engine cowlings and rudder. Broad white fuselage band and extreme end of tail. 'K' of code is also in RLM 27, outlined in black. Note thin black line on spinner

✠ **Heinkel He 111H-3, S7+HA, Geschwaderstab St.G 3, Derna (North Africa), September 1941**
RLM 79 on top surfaces with RLM 78 Hellblau undersurfaces. White fuselage band and undersides of wingtips; RLM 24 spinner and individual letter 'H' on fuselage, the latter repeated in black under the wings

✠ **Heinkel He 111P-4, VG+ES, of Korpskette X, Fliegerkorps, Western Desert, winter 1941-42**
RLM 79 upper surfaces with mottling of (probably) RLM 71 and RLM 65 undersides. White underside of wingtips, spinners and a wide rear fuselage band. Note how the 'E' and part of the 'S' of the code are outlined in black, to make them stand out against the background

✠ **Junkers Ju 52/3m g4e, 4U+NH, allocated to 2. (F)/123, Derna, June 1941**
RLM 79/80/78 scheme with RLM 70/71 rudder and starboard flap upper surfaces. White rear fuselage band

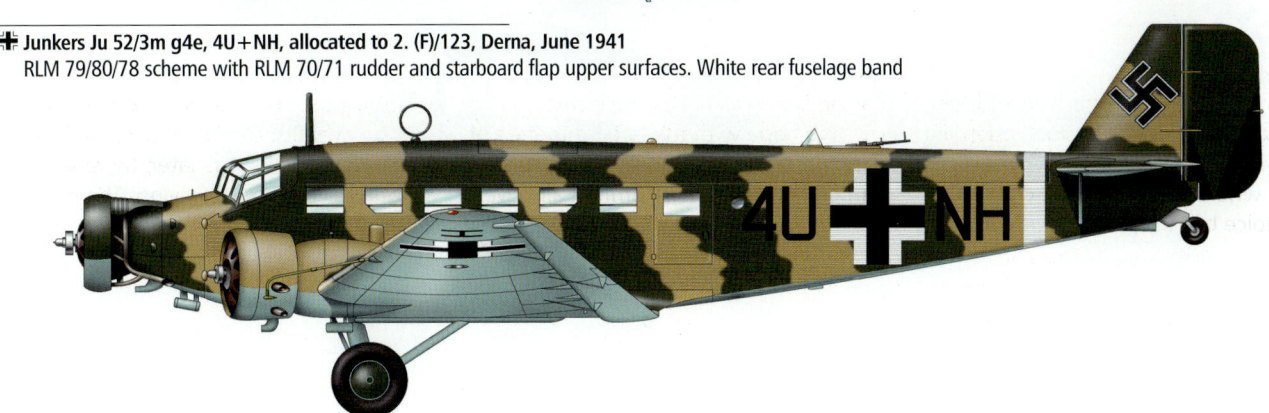

✠ **Messerschmitt Bf 109E-7/Trop, 'Black 3', 2./JG 27, Gazala, spring 1941**
RLM 74/75 upper surfaces with RLM 76 undersides and fuselage sides; overpainting is probably in RLM 70 or RLM 71 on the fuselage and tail area.
Red/white spinner, black '3' outlined in red

✠ **Messerschmitt Bf 109E-7/Trop, flown by Hptm Eduard Neumann, commander of I./JG 27, Gazala, May 1941**
RLM 75/75 upper surfaces with RLM 76 undersides; yellow nose and rudder. RLM 70 spinner.
Black chevrons, outlined in white, on fuselage sides.
Eight victory markings on rudder

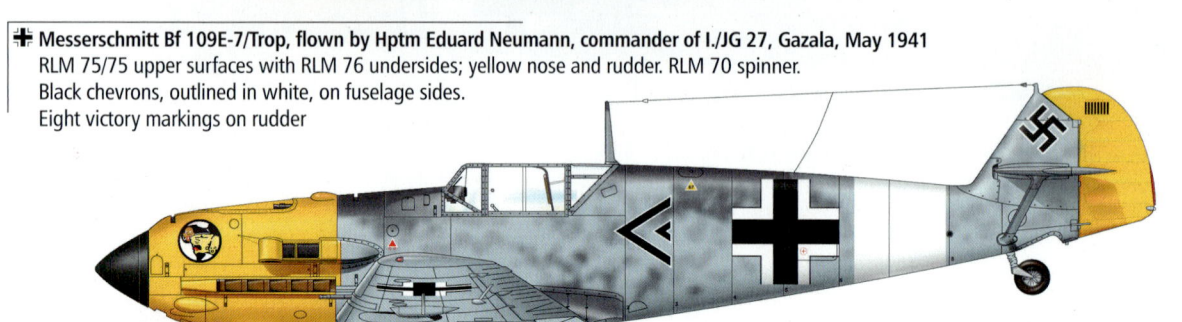

✠ **Messerschmitt Bf 109F-4/Z/Trop, W/Nr.8580, 'Yellow 1', flown by Staffelkapitän Hptm. Gerald Homuth, 3./JG 27, Martuba, April 1942**
RLM 79 on all the top surfaces with RLM 78 undersides. White nose, rear fuselage band and underside of wingtips. Yellow '1', outlined in black.
Yellow victory bars on rudder. See also top view

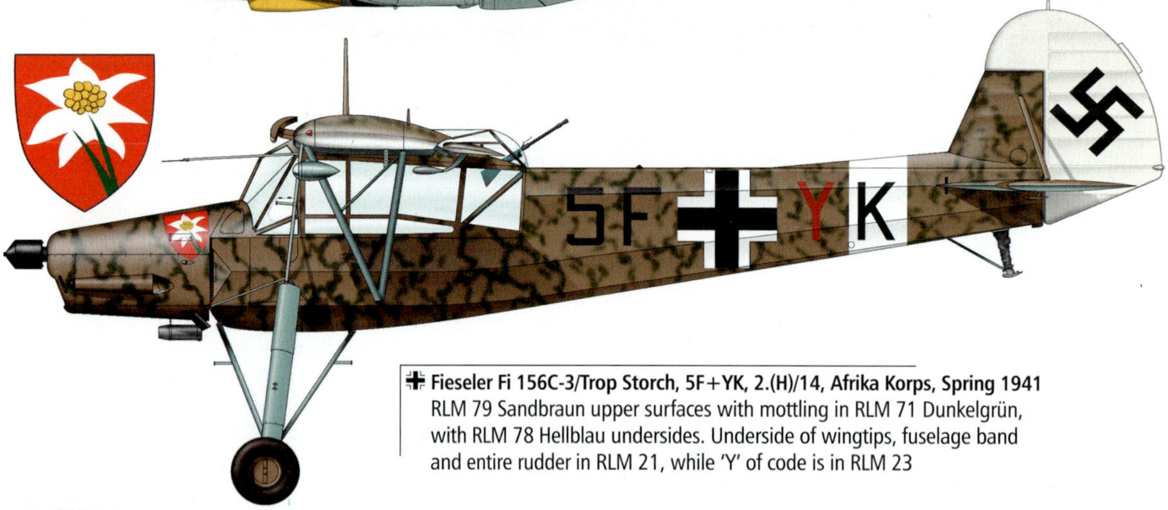

✠ **Fieseler Fi 156C-3/Trop Storch, 5F+YK, 2.(H)/14, Afrika Korps, Spring 1941**
RLM 79 Sandbraun upper surfaces with mottling in RLM 71 Dunkelgrün, with RLM 78 Hellblau undersides. Underside of wingtips, fuselage band and entire rudder in RLM 21, while 'Y' of code is in RLM 23

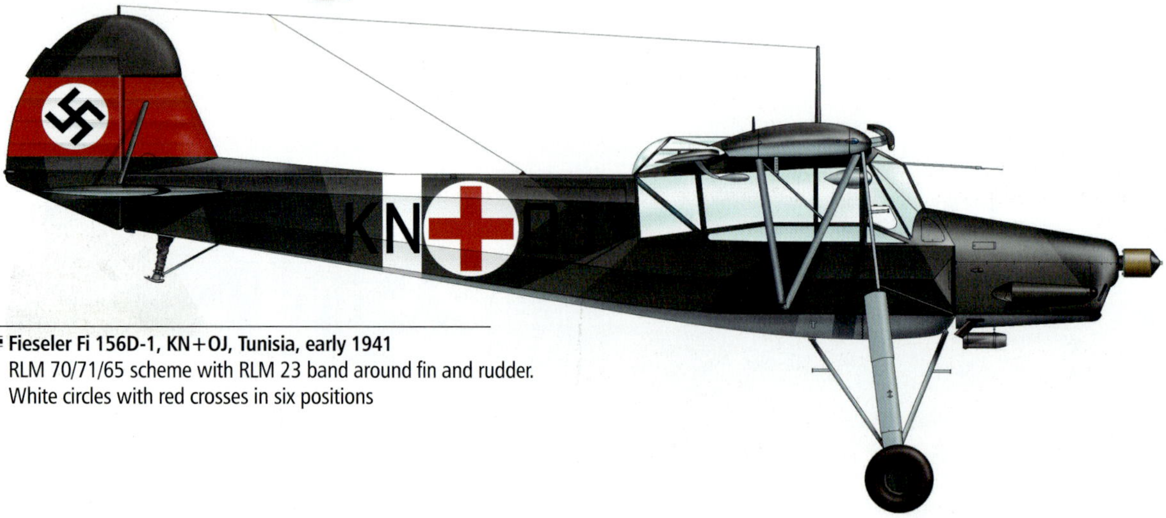

✠ **Fieseler Fi 156D-1, KN+OJ, Tunisia, early 1941**
RLM 70/71/65 scheme with RLM 23 band around fin and rudder.
White circles with red crosses in six positions

Luftwaffe Colour Profiles – © Richard J. Caruana 2018

✠ **Henschel Hs 126B-1/Trop, 5F+CK, 2.(H)/14, Libya, 1942**
Standard RLM 70/71 upper surfaces overpainted in RLM 79 and undersides in RLM 65.
White rear fuselage band; codes in black. Unit badge with blue background on nose

✠ **Henschel Hs 129B-2, W/Nr.0278, 'Red X', 8.(Pz)Sch.G 2, El Aouina (Tunisia), early 1943**
RLM 79 uppersurfaces with mottles in RLM 80 and RLM 78 undersides.
White rear fuselage band and undersides of wingtips. Red 'X', painted
over the previous blue 'X' (slightly faded giving a purple appearance)
outlined in white

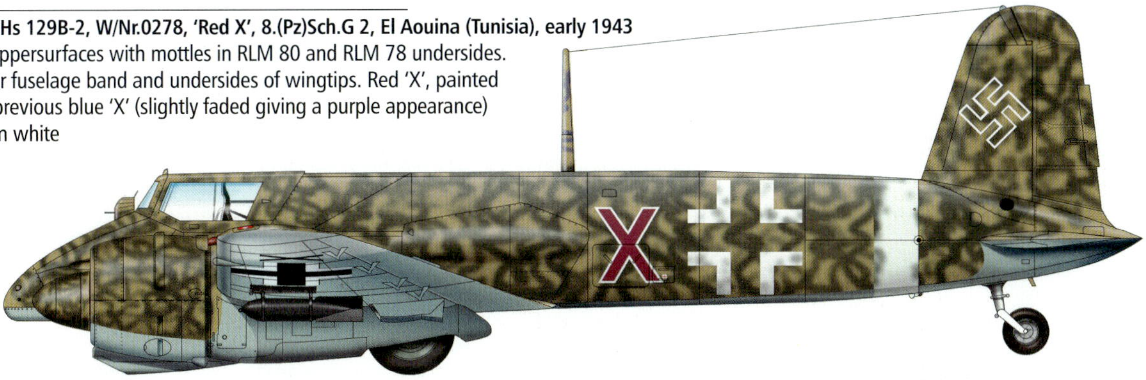

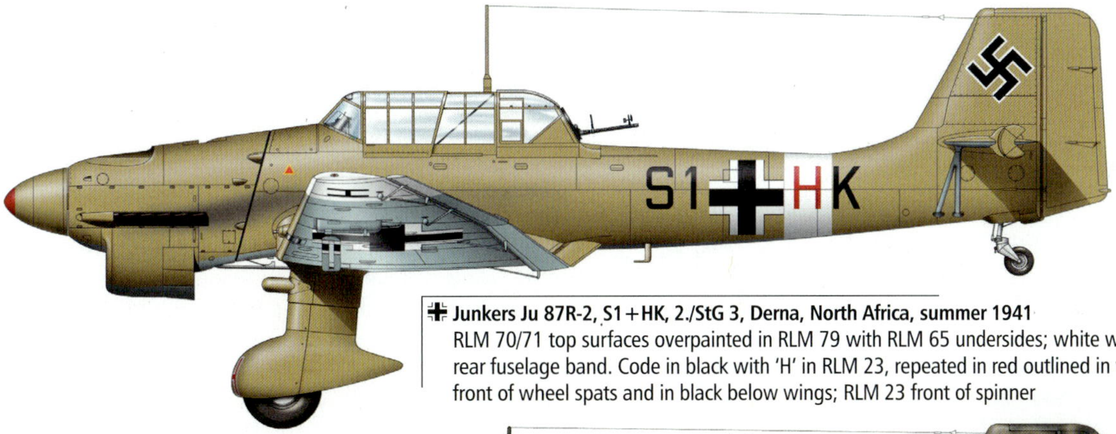

✠ **Junkers Ju 87R-2, S1+HK, 2./StG 3, Derna, North Africa, summer 1941**
RLM 70/71 top surfaces overpainted in RLM 79 with RLM 65 undersides; white wingtips and
rear fuselage band. Code in black with 'H' in RLM 23, repeated in red outlined in white on
front of wheel spats and in black below wings; RLM 23 front of spinner

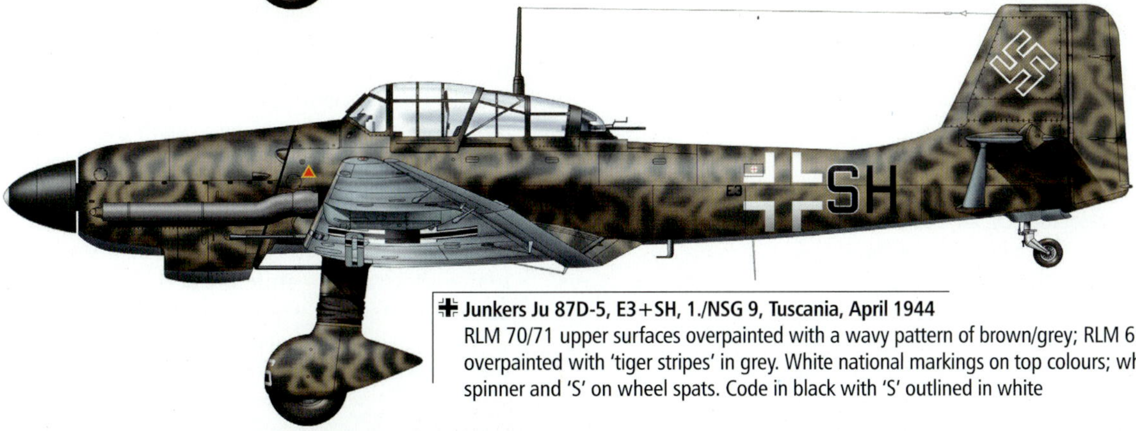

✠ **Junkers Ju 87D-5, E3+SH, 1./NSG 9, Tuscania, April 1944**
RLM 70/71 upper surfaces overpainted with a wavy pattern of brown/grey; RLM 65 undersides also
overpainted with 'tiger stripes' in grey. White national markings on top colours; white extreme tip of
spinner and 'S' on wheel spats. Code in black with 'S' outlined in white

✠ **Junkers Ju 88D-4/Trop, B3+BL, I/KG 54, Gerbini (Sicily), April 1942**
RLM 70/71 uppersurfaces with addition of RLM 79 and RLM 65 undersides. RLM 04 spinner, underside of
cowling and 'B' of code

Kittyhawk Mk Ia

1/72nd
by Libor Jekl

The popularity of the P-40 has been reflected by kit manufacturers over the years, so modellers could choose from a decent range in all main scales. In 1/72nd scale we had the Hasegawa and Academy kits that dealt with the demand for quite some time. However, it did not mean they were not without faults, especially the Academy offering, which suffered from substantial shape issues. Fortunately, times have changed and we now have a brand new kit of the Kittyhawk Mk Ia along with the P-40N that was released simultaneously by Special Hobby. At this point it is necessary to point out these kits do not have anything in common with the P-40F released couple of years ago, although that is quite a decent kit and the only reasonable choice for an F in this scale. The Kittyhawk Mk Ia kit consists of about seventy parts moulded from a grey-coloured plastic spread out on two sprues. The first one is obviously common for all their P-40 kits and it contains optional parts such as instrument panels, seats, backrests, propellers, main wheels, exhausts plus other smaller pieces, while the second sprue provides the base components for the wing, tailplanes and fuselage. All parts are cleanly moulded with sharp panel lines and other surface details like fasteners, caps or hatches, while some of them are slightly protruding from the surface when that is applicable. The fabric effect on the control surfaces is also subtly done with sharply defined ribs that may again help to accentuate these details at the painting stage. I like the realistically deep separation of the control surfaces as well, especially those underneath the ailerons, which perfectly match the real thing. The cockpit is provided as a multiple part assembly with separately moulded sidewalls, instrument panel with raised dials (you can use a decal instead), seat with its tubular structure and others. The compound radiator section in the nose also looks very busy with the individual oil and liquid radiator bodies depicted and the control flaps can be

The Special Hobby kit box

Technical Data	
Special Hobby 1/72nd Curtiss Kittyhawk Mk Ia	
Kit No.: SH72377	Material: IM
Manufacturer: Special Hobby, Czech Republic	
UK Price: £13.60	

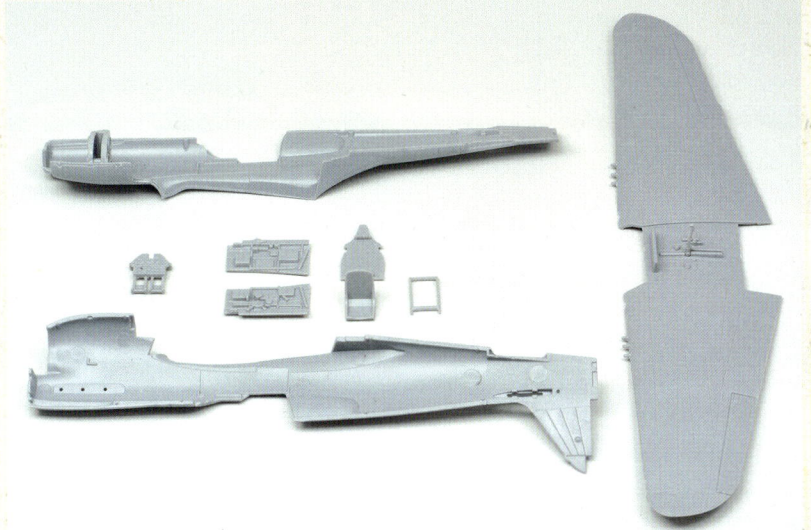

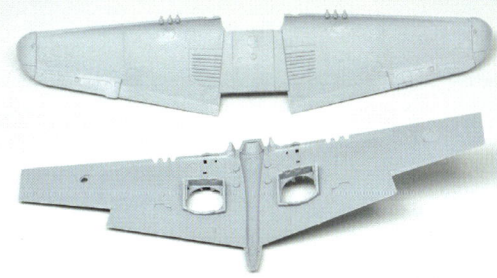

The wings feature nice fabric effect on the ailerons, and the wheel wells use separate parts to box them in, as well as corrugations moulded into the inside of the upper wing half

Cockpit interior detail is quite nice straight from the box, note the 'floor' section built into the upper wing half, as is the case with the real aircraft

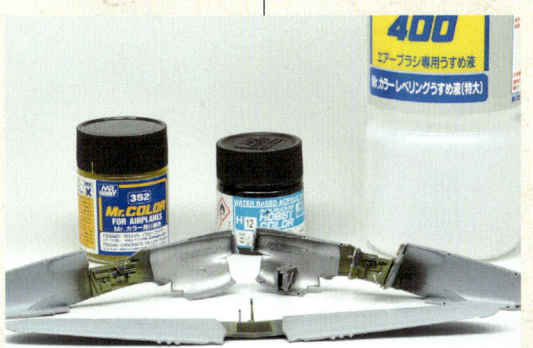

The front region of the fuselage is sprayed aluminium, whilst the cockpit interior uses Chromate Yellow with a touch of black to darken it

The overall level of detail is good, the only additions here being the seat belts from the Eduard set

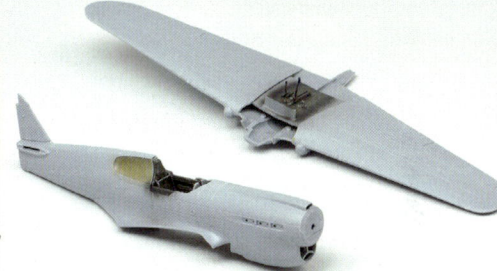

The fuselage and wings assembled, note that the gun barrels moulded to the wing leading edges have been sanded off which is because the option chosen by Libor did not have these fairings

The wing root joint is pretty good on the upper surface, just a bit of filler needed to close the gap

Clamps were needed on the underside though, just to ensure the central 'tunnel' fairing all lines up

New holes for the guns were drilled into the leading edge of each wing

The rudder is separate, so this results in a nice deep and convincing hinge line

The areas underneath the clear panels aft of the cockpit are sprayed with Middle Stone

The windscreen is actually the first clear piece to be secured

Then the clear panels can be positioned and secured with a bit of PVA

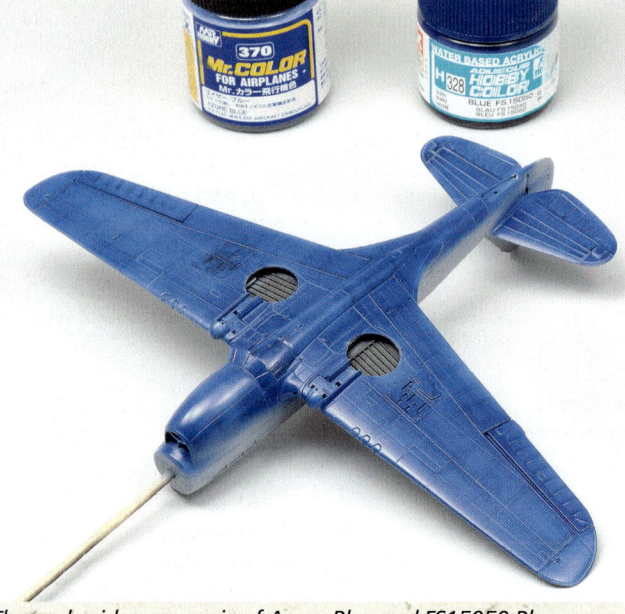

All areas that would suffer from wear are first primed with Alclad 2 Aluminium, then hairspray is applied over the top

The undersides are a mix of Azure Blue and FS15050 Blue

posed open or closed. The separately moulded air inlet features individual ducts running to each cooler section, however they are only schematic and a bit short. Fortunately this is not a problem on the finished kit and I guess they come about purely down to one of tooling cost; it also makes assembly at lot easier. Many delicate details can be found in the wheel bays where the sidewalls are moulded separately and the roofs contain the typical corrugations of the type. The landing gear legs look very nice along with their tie rods and covers. The wheels are provided with either plain or spoked hubs, although the latter are obviously intended for later P-40 versions. The kit also contains two styles of drop tanks and a bomb, although this is intended more for the USAAF versions I suspect. Anyway, modellers wishing to add even more details can use the resin sets that were released at the same time as the kit in the CMK and Quick & Easy ranges, such as the Cockpit Sidewall and Control Column set (#Q72301), Undercarriage set (#7389), Control Surfaces set (#7386), Seat with Belts set (#Q72299), Armament set (#7386) or Wheels set with diamond, block, or cross-ply tread patterns (#Q72295, #Q72296 and #Q72297). They also offer British GP 250lb bombs (#7343) suitable for any RAF Kittyhawk. The kit's transparencies are also of a very high standard being clear and thin and you have the central region separate, which allows you to pose it in the open position. The instructions are printed on glossy paper in colour and the twelve clear construction steps should guide you through the building and painting stages, the latter having all paint references to Gunze-Sangyo Mr Color and Mr Aqueous Color ranges. The decal sheet is printed by Cartograf and is of excellent quality; it provides markings for AK772 'London Pride' from No.112 Squadron, Libya 1942; A-29-153 of No.75 Squadron RAAF based in New Guinea in 1943, and AK905 of No.111(F) Squadron RCAF operating in 1942 from Anchorage, Alaska.

The Middle Stone on the upper surfaces is lightened slightly with a creamy colour

The final colour to go on the upper surfaces is Dark Earth

Construction

I started off with installation of the radiator bodies in the nose, which were glued together from a couple of identical pieces, so that the screens can be seen from both the inlet and outlet. I prepared the cockpit parts next along with the wing's upper half that contains the cockpit floor similarly to the real thing. The inner sides of the nose were sprayed Aluminium (Alclad II ALC-102), while the interior colour was mixed from H12 Black and Mr Color 352 Chromate Yellow; according to the instructions you may wish to consider adding a drop of brown because the Interior Green used by Curtiss showed a slight brownish tint to it. At the same time I also airbrushed the wheel well sidewalls that were then glued to the wing's bottom half. The seat belts were sourced from Eduard's set (#73036), the cockpit details were picked out in Vallejo acrylics and further dry-brushed with light grey to accentuate their contours. Trial assembly of the fuselage and wing went satisfactorily because all the joints matched with minimum tolerances, so they could be secured with a few passes of extra thin Mr Cement S. Only on the bottom area did I have to use some clamps to ensure the correct position of the ventral fairing over the rear fuselage. The machine I was building does not seem to have had the gun fairings on the wing leading edge (maybe these were temporarily removed?), so I sanded them off with a flat sanding stick. Next I redrilled the openings for the gun barrels, noting that the mid gun was placed slightly above the outer guns. The wing-to-fuselage joint was next cleaned up and I continued with the addition of the tailplanes and rudder. The latter item is moulded separately so it can be easily inserted in the slots thus creating a realistically deep gap with openings for the elevator push rods. The manufacturer forgot to depict a small hole for cockpit ventilation in the starboard wing root fairing, so I drilled this using a 1mm drill bit. I

The leading edges of the mid/outer wing panels are masked and sprayed yellow

An old brush, moistened with warm water, is then used to scrub off some of the paint to expose the aluminium underneath

The oil panel wash on the upper surfaces is based on brown shades

The oil wash on the undersides, however, uses sand and cream shades

The wheels once painted receive some pastel dust from the MIG Productions range

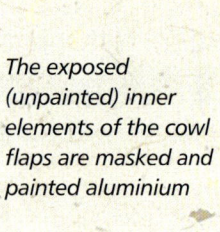

The sharkmouth decal under the nose fits well, but some touching up with red and black acrylics is still needed

The exposed (unpainted) inner elements of the cowl flaps are masked and painted aluminium

used the extended version of the radiator control flaps, however on their inside I discovered a small ejector pin mark that had to be filled with thicker cyanoacrylate, plus you may also wish to add the linkage operating the flaps made from stretched sprue. The area beneath the fuselage side windows was airbrushed Middle Stone so that I could cement in situ the clear parts. Before installing the windshield it is necessary to cover the instrument panel with its fairing; note however that this part seemed to be removed on some Kittyhawks. This was a leather cover that was often left partially or completely removed for easier maintenance, in which case you would need to add some cabling and rear faces to all the (now) visible instruments. The side windows literally snapped into the fuselage openings, so I secured them with a small amount of Gator Grip white glue instead of cyanoacrylate to avoid fogging the parts. The main transparencies were next, masked off using Eduard's pre-cut masks (#CX501) and after the base coat of Mr Surfacer 1000 (grey) was applied I airbrushed the kit's surface with Alclad II Aluminium as a primer coat for the subsequent painting and weathering stages.

Colour & Markings

Kittyhawk AK772 had the undersides apparently painted in a darker colour than the regular Azure Blue; the instructions recommend Dark Mediterranean Blue, while other sources mention Deep Sky as an alternative. I decided that the H328 blue listed in the instructions was as good a base for the Dark Mediterranean Blue, however I made it slightly brighter with the addition of about 50% Azure Blue (Mr Color 370) because the paint used directly from the bottle looked just too dark. On the upper surfaces I applied a few layers of hairspray as the base for paint chipping technique and then continued with Middle Stone H71, which on the real aircraft was sprayed over the original Dark Green areas. H71 seemed to be too orange-yellow for my tastes when used straight from the bottle, so I modified it with the addition of about 20%

The 250lb GP British bomb came from the spares box, as the kit only has a American-style bomb in it. The cast effect for the body was created by using a sponge to roughly apply Mr Surfacer 500

H85 Sail to give it a more appropriate sandy hue. Next I airbrushed the remaining Dark Earth (H72) with a soft demarcation between the two, masked off the wing leading edges and applied H24 Yellow over them.

Now I could move on to the more fun part of the painting, the weathering. I soaked an old brush with cut hairs in hot water and applied it over those parts of the airframe subject to wear, such as the leading edges, wing roots and around various access panels. The water reacted with the hairspray layer underneath and the paint peeled off, showing the Aluminium base coat. On the Middle Stone patches I also brushed on some scratches of the original Dark Green using a fine brush and the surface was next sealed with gloss varnish GX100.

The decals performed very well, they showed great opacity and perfectly conformed to the panel lines. The complex sharkmouth motif was split into three parts and it eventually settled down nicely too, although I had to retouch it in places with red and black acrylics. The serial number was already printed with the surrounding Dark Green rectangle, so you do not have to bother with any additional masking and painting prior to applying it.

On the wing undersides I applied an oil wash mixed from sand and creamy shades, while on upper sides I used more brown and black. The final painting job was to mask off and airbrush the inner elements of the radiator outlet flaps in Aluminium.

Once suitably painted and the rack is modified, the bomb looks most effective in situ

The new gun barrels were made from tubing; note that the inner guns project less than the outer one

Final Details

From the kit I used the wheels with the smooth tread, which AK772 apparently had, and after painting them H77 Tyre Black the hubs were gently dusted with a sand-coloured pigment from the MIG Productions range. The 250lb bomb I eventually found in my spares box and using a piece of sponge I stippled it with Mr Surfacer 500, thus imitating the rough surface of the cast iron, and then painted it Dark Green with a yellow/cream tail; the bomb rack mounting was modified from the kit parts. From the Albion Alloys range I cut a set of six barrels, which once the fairings were removed, simply projected from the wing leading edges. The kit does not provide the British style cranked pitot probe, but at least a diagram is provided in the instructions as a guide for scratchbuilding one. From my spares I also added the external gunsights in front of the windshield, these coming from an old generic photo-etched set. At the very end I installed the canopy centre section, propeller and the aerials running from the fin to the spine and port wing.

Verdict

Special Hobby kits have always belonged to the better part of the short-run element in the market. With the recent changes there resulting in Special Hobby being an independent brand there are also significant changes in the kit design and production. After the first very promising signs with their Mirage F.1 kits we now have a high quality P-40 kit that can be considered as one of the best on the market, providing a great amount of detail, and a delicate and tidy surface. Its well thought out design allows Special Hobby to cover other P-40 versions without compromising fit due to having to use odd splits and breaks in the main components; for instance each specific version will be provided with a new fuselage, so no separate noses or tails to deal with. We can therefore look forward to variants, which thus far have never appeared as an accurate state-of-the-art kit, such as the 'long tail' P-40K or M.

Paints Used
Alclad II lacquer:
ALC-102 Aluminium
Gunze-Sangyo Mr Color lacquer:
C370 Azure Blue
C352 Chromate Yellow
GX100 Super Clear Gloss
Gunze-Sangyo Mr Aqueous Color acrylic:
H12 Black   H24 Yellow
H71 Middle Stone   H72 Dark Earth
H77 Tyre Black   H85 Sail
Gunze-Sangyo Mr Finishing Surfacer 1500 (Black)
Gunze-Sangyo Mr Surfacer 1000 (Grey)

References
- Curtiss P-40 Kittyhawk I-IV by R. Wagner, Profile No.136 (Profile Publications 1967)
- Kittyhawk Mk I/Ia, Model Detail Photo Monograph No.14 (Rossagraph 2004 ISBN: 83-919061-6-7)
- P-40 Warhawk Part 1 [P-36 to P-40C] by B. Kinsey, Detail & Scale Vol.61 (Squadron/Signal Publications 1999 ISBN: 1-888974-14-1)

- Spitfire, Mustang and Kittyhawk in Australian Servbice by S. Wilson (Aerospace Publications Pty Ltd 1988 ISBN: 0-9587978-1-1)
- Tomahawk and Kittyhawk Aces of the RAF and Commonwealth, Osprey Aircraft of the Aces No.38 (Osprey Publishing 2003)

Historical Significance

Everyone knows the P-40 and so they should, as it was one of the true heroes of WWII. Never mind that it didn't get to bask in the limelight of its more glamorous stable mates, this was the true workhorse. The British used the original P-40B/C under the name Tomahawk and when Curtiss redesigned it to take the more powerful Allison engine they took it under their wing as the Kittyhawk. The Mk Ia version is roughly equivalent to the American P-40E but with the addition of British radio gear and equipment. It's this aircraft that gained No.112 Squadron such fame and notoriety in the North African Campaign. This was the first unit to carry the famous 'Shark Mouth' design, carried over onto their new machines from the older Tomahawks. As a pure fighter, the Kittyhawk was not really a match for the brand new Bf 109F but it was fast and rugged, being famous for the strength of the airframe and its ability to adapt to new roles. It really came into its own as a fighter-bomber, with bombs slung under the wings and fuselage it provided much needed support to the troops on the desert sand. Used by not only the RAF but also the South African Air Force, it was well liked by both air and ground crews because it was such a strong aircraft. Its greatest use came around the fighting for El Alamein, where the aircraft and squadron really showed their mettle, with almost constant strikes against the German Afrika Korps. The Kittyhawk Mk Ias soon gave way to the even more powerful Mk IIs and Mk IIIs and they were kept in constant use right up until No.112 Squadron re-equipped with Mustangs for the final push into Italy. Many of the surplus Kittyhawks found their way into French service where they served once more in the desert heat of Tunisia and Algiers.

◉ **Hawker Hurricane Mk IId, BP188, JV•Z, No.6 Squadron, June 1942**
Dark Earth/Mid Stone/Azure Blue finish with black spinner; 'JV' code in
Medium Sea Grey, 'Z' in gloss red. Standard national
markings; serial in black

◉ **Hawker Hurricane Mk.IIc, BP592, AK•G, of No.213 Squadron, El Alamein (Western Desert), 1942**
Dark Earth/Mid Stone/Azure Blue finish, with squiggle camouflage applied to cowling
area and wing leading edges over Mid Stone; codes in white,
serial in black. Standard national markings

◉ **Hawker Hurricane Mk IIb, HL795, •V, No.274 Squadron, summer 1942**
Dark Earth/Mid-Stone upper surfaces with Azure Blue undersides. Red spinner,
Night serial, White code 'V'. Blue flash across fuselage roundel

◉ **Hawker Hurricane Mk IIb, BD930, FG•Σ, No.335 (Hellenic) Squadron, LG.85 (Western Desert), October 1943**
Dark Earth/Mid Stone/Azure Blue scheme with white codes and black serial;
red of national markings on fuselage sides, below wings and
fin flash overpainted in blue. Mid-blue/white spinner

◉ **Hawker Hurricane Mk XIIb built by Canadian Car & Foundry (converted to Sea Hurricane), JS327,
No.800 Naval Air Squadron FAA, November 1942**
Extra Dark Sea Grey/Dark Slate Grey upper surfaces with Sky undersides. Red spinner, lettering in Night.
British national markings overpainted with US star marking in six positions, those above wings and
on fuselage sides having a yellow outline. Crash-landed on the beach at St. Leu,
in Algeria during Torch landings, 8th November 1942

- **Tomahawk Mk IIB, AK354, GA•L, No.112 Squadron RAF, North Africa, October 1941**
  Dark Earth/Mid Stone/Azure Blue finish. Red spinner and light grey codes

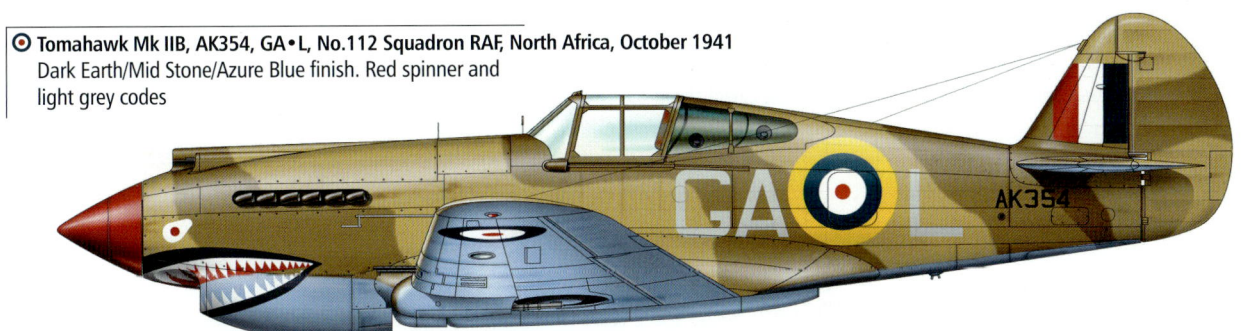

- **Curtiss Kittyhawk Mk I, AK673, GA•F, No.112 Squadron, No.239 Wing, North Africa**
  Dark Earth/Mid Stone upper surfaces with Azure Blue undersides; red spinner, red/white/black sharkmouth motif around nose air intake. Codes in white, serial in Night

- **Curtiss Kittyhawk Mk Ia, ET789, GA•C, flown by Sgt Hogg (SAAF), No.112 Squadron, No.239 Wing, LG91, Amriyha (Egypt), October 1942**
  Dark Earth/Mid-Stone/Azure Blue finish with white codes and Night serials; red spinner. Red/white sharkmouth motif, outlined in black

- **Brewster Buffalo Mk I, AS420, 'Z', No.805 Naval Air Squadron (FAA), Egypt, Early 1941**
  Dark Earth/Dark Green upper surfaces with Sky undersides; Night spinner and code on fuselage, the latter repeated in white on front of cowling. Squadron badge on forward fuselage

- **Gloster Gladiator Mk II, GK•Z, of No.80 Squadron, Egypt early 1940**
  Dark Earth and Dark Green upper surfaces. Black/white undersides of fuselage and lower wings only; underside of upper wings up to this time remained unpainted. Note attempt to tone down earlier 'bright' identification colours on fuselage roundel

- **Supermarine Spitfire Mk Vb, EP841, UF•F, No.601 Squadron, North Africa, summer 1943**
  Dark Earth and Mid-Stone upper surfaces with Azure Blue undersides. Codes are white. Standard markings, including type B roundels above wings. Note squadron 'Winged Sword' in a white circle, above the fin flash and 'Abouqir' filter

- **Supermarine Spitfire Mk Vb, ER773, No.33 Squadron, Bersis (Libya), 1943**
  Dark Earth and Mid-Stone upper surfaces with Azure Blue undersides.
  Codes and serial in Night. Red spinner

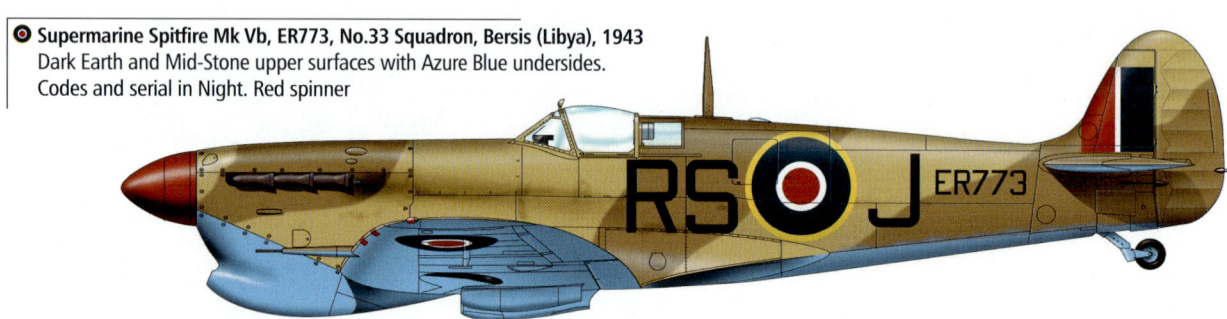

- **Supermarine Spitfire Mk VIII, JF814, •WFD, flown by Air Vice Marshal Sir William F. Dickson, AOC Desert Air Force, April 1944**
  Dark Earth and Mid-Stone upper surfaces with Azure Blue undersides. Red initials on fuselage sides outlined in white.
  Serial in Night. AVM pennant below windscreen, red spinner

- **Supermarine Spitfire Mk IX, EN298, RN•B, flown by Flt Lt D.G.S.R. Cox, No.72 Squadron, Algeria, spring 1943**
  Dark Earth and Mid Stone upper surfaces with Azure Blue undersides.
  Codes and spinner in red, serial in Night. 'PAT' in white below windscreen

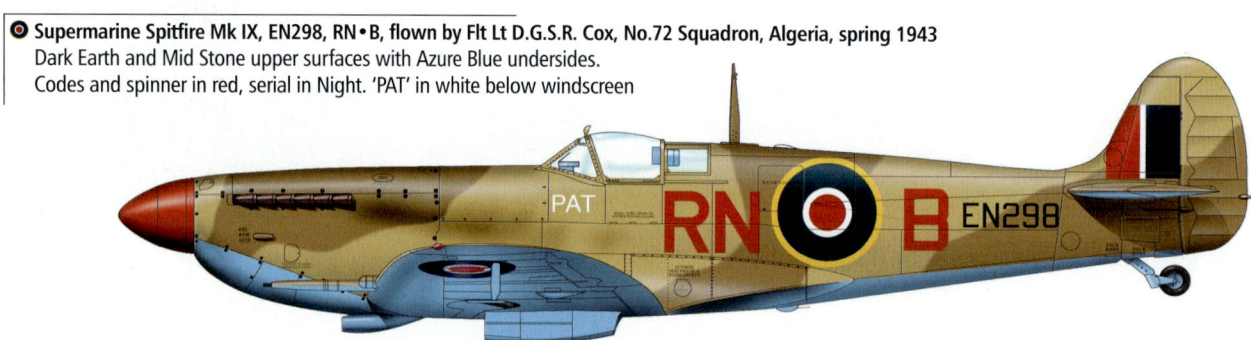

- **Hawker Typhoon Mk Ib, R8925, •B, during tropical trials, Ismalia, early 1943**
  Dark Earth and Mid-Stone upper surfaces, Azzure Blue undersides.
  Standard markings in all positions, except for yellow wing
  leading edge; red spinner

RAF-Commonwealth Colour Profiles – © Richard J. Caruana 2018   Airframe Extra No.9 – North Africa Campaign

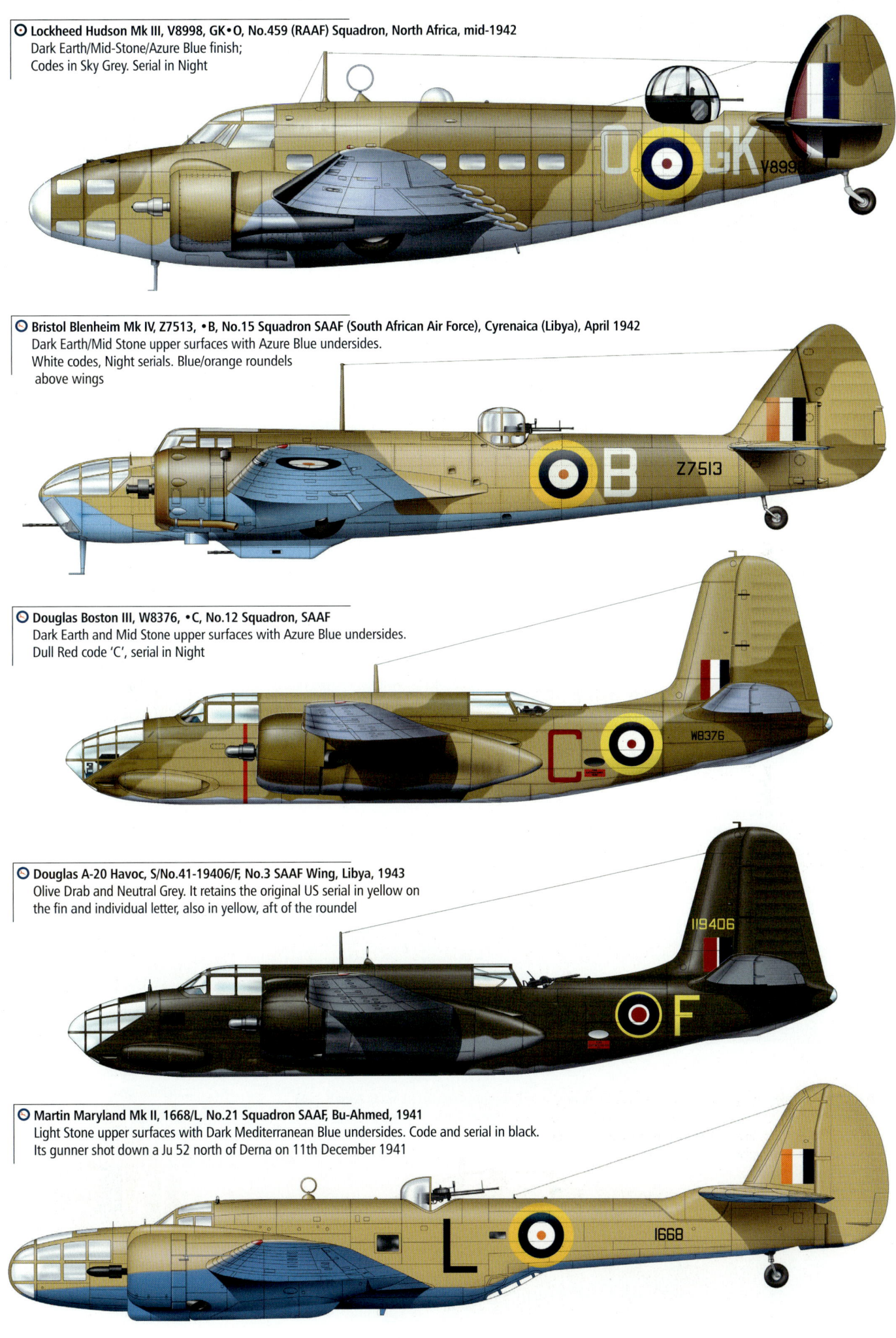

- **Lockheed Hudson Mk III, V8998, GK•O, No.459 (RAAF) Squadron, North Africa, mid-1942**
  Dark Earth/Mid-Stone/Azure Blue finish;
  Codes in Sky Grey. Serial in Night

- **Bristol Blenheim Mk IV, Z7513, •B, No.15 Squadron SAAF (South African Air Force), Cyrenaica (Libya), April 1942**
  Dark Earth/Mid Stone upper surfaces with Azure Blue undersides.
  White codes, Night serials. Blue/orange roundels
  above wings

- **Douglas Boston III, W8376, •C, No.12 Squadron, SAAF**
  Dark Earth and Mid Stone upper surfaces with Azure Blue undersides.
  Dull Red code 'C', serial in Night

- **Douglas A-20 Havoc, S/No.41-19406/F, No.3 SAAF Wing, Libya, 1943**
  Olive Drab and Neutral Grey. It retains the original US serial in yellow on
  the fin and individual letter, also in yellow, aft of the roundel

- **Martin Maryland Mk II, 1668/L, No.21 Squadron SAAF, Bu-Ahmed, 1941**
  Light Stone upper surfaces with Dark Mediterranean Blue undersides. Code and serial in black.
  Its gunner shot down a Ju 52 north of Derna on 11th December 1941

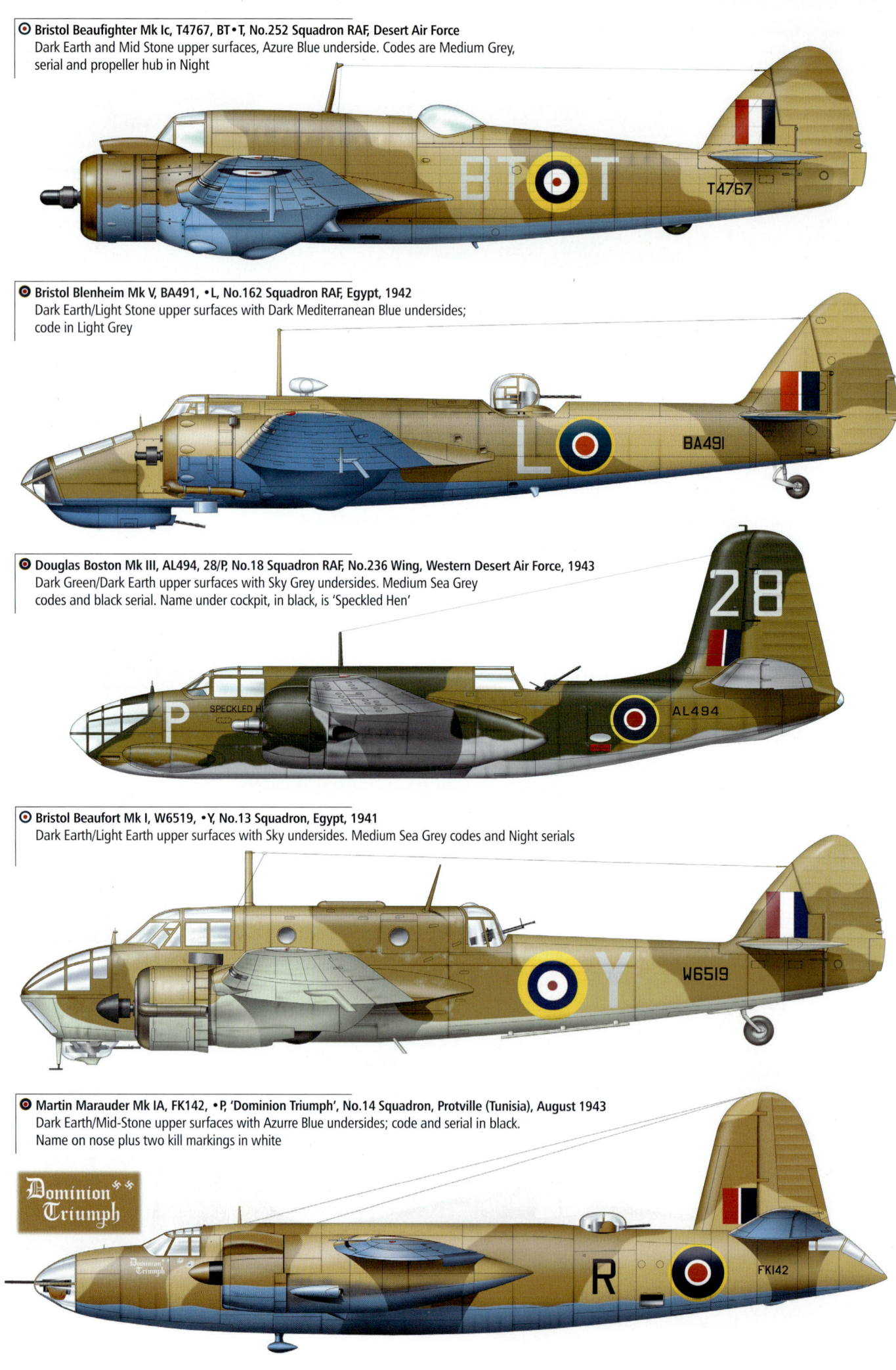

- **Bristol Beaufighter Mk Ic, T4767, BT•T, No.252 Squadron RAF, Desert Air Force**
  Dark Earth and Mid Stone upper surfaces, Azure Blue underside. Codes are Medium Grey, serial and propeller hub in Night

- **Bristol Blenheim Mk V, BA491, •L, No.162 Squadron RAF, Egypt, 1942**
  Dark Earth/Light Stone upper surfaces with Dark Mediterranean Blue undersides; code in Light Grey

- **Douglas Boston Mk III, AL494, 28/P, No.18 Squadron RAF, No.236 Wing, Western Desert Air Force, 1943**
  Dark Green/Dark Earth upper surfaces with Sky Grey undersides. Medium Sea Grey codes and black serial. Name under cockpit, in black, is 'Speckled Hen'

- **Bristol Beaufort Mk I, W6519, •Y, No.13 Squadron, Egypt, 1941**
  Dark Earth/Light Earth upper surfaces with Sky undersides. Medium Sea Grey codes and Night serials

- **Martin Marauder Mk IA, FK142, •P, 'Dominion Triumph', No.14 Squadron, Protville (Tunisia), August 1943**
  Dark Earth/Mid-Stone upper surfaces with Azurre Blue undersides; code and serial in black. Name on nose plus two kill markings in white

RAF-Commonwealth Colour Profiles – © Richard J. Caruana 2018   Airframe Extra No.9 – North Africa Campaign

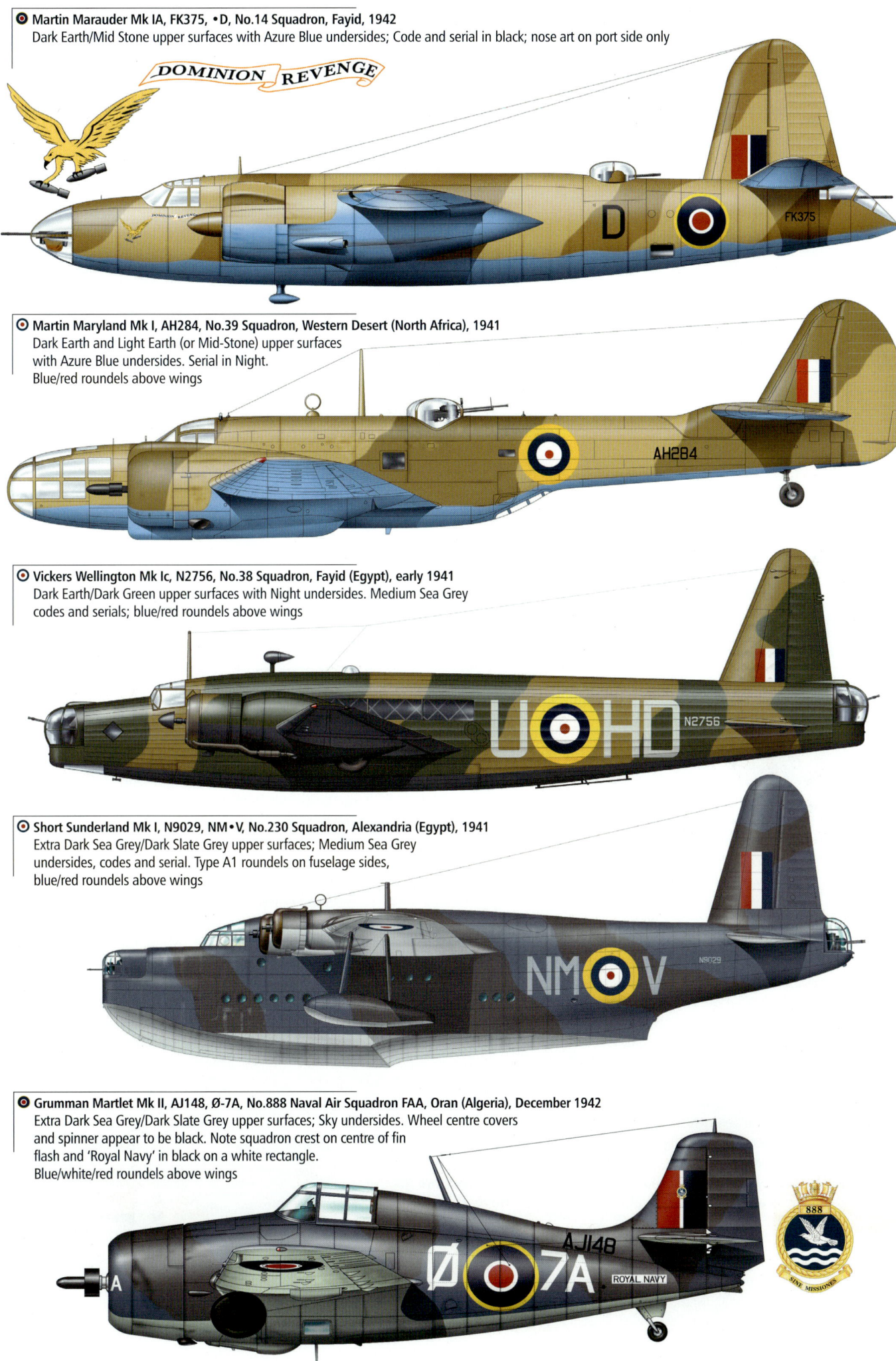

- **Martin Marauder Mk IA, FK375, •D, No.14 Squadron, Fayid, 1942**
  Dark Earth/Mid Stone upper surfaces with Azure Blue undersides; Code and serial in black; nose art on port side only

- **Martin Maryland Mk I, AH284, No.39 Squadron, Western Desert (North Africa), 1941**
  Dark Earth and Light Earth (or Mid-Stone) upper surfaces with Azure Blue undersides. Serial in Night. Blue/red roundels above wings

- **Vickers Wellington Mk Ic, N2756, No.38 Squadron, Fayid (Egypt), early 1941**
  Dark Earth/Dark Green upper surfaces with Night undersides. Medium Sea Grey codes and serials; blue/red roundels above wings

- **Short Sunderland Mk I, N9029, NM•V, No.230 Squadron, Alexandria (Egypt), 1941**
  Extra Dark Sea Grey/Dark Slate Grey upper surfaces; Medium Sea Grey undersides, codes and serial. Type A1 roundels on fuselage sides, blue/red roundels above wings

- **Grumman Martlet Mk II, AJ148, Ø-7A, No.888 Naval Air Squadron FAA, Oran (Algeria), December 1942**
  Extra Dark Sea Grey/Dark Slate Grey upper surfaces; Sky undersides. Wheel centre covers and spinner appear to be black. Note squadron crest on centre of fin flash and 'Royal Navy' in black on a white rectangle. Blue/white/red roundels above wings

Hurricane Mk IId

1/32nd
by Steve A. Evans

Why has it taken this long to get a Hurricane in a modern moulding in this scale? Isn't this machine one of the all time greats? Isn't it one of the most important aircraft in RAF history? Isn't it gorgeous in every way? Well, OK, maybe gorgeous isn't the right word to describe this iconic machine but it's not as if it's ugly and it was vitally important to the RAF during the Battle of Britain. Admittedly it was outclassed and outshone by its stablemate Spitfire, but finding other uses for the Hurricane gave it a whole new lease of life in service. Fly have finally given the modelling world an up-to-date moulding, mostly in plastic but with the addition of a few resin parts and a small etched fret. It all nestles in a large box with some dashing art on the lid. You can chose between no fewer than seven different versions as well, which is an excellent move from Fly. The plastic in the box comes on five large sprues, in a sand-ish kind of colour, with various parts not used on this mark. The plastic is very well detailed, although a little rough round the edges with lots of flash and mould lines. If you have ever built an earlier Special Hobby kit, it's got that kind of feeling to it. There are plenty of ejector pin marks and some clumsy sprue gates to deal with as well but it's not too bad and easy enough for even an inexperienced modeller to deal with. The detail is good throughout, with lots of external raised bits and recessed panel lines where appropriate. They have attempted to show the rivets as close to the real thing as possible as well, where much of the outer wing sections were constructed with mushroom head rivets and not countersunk. This will not please some people who don't like the 'riveted' look but I think it suits the slightly old-fashioned style of the real thing. The resin parts are OK,

The box is big and sturdy, like the aircraft itself, with some neat art on the top and sides. I always like to see the marking options on the box

Technical Data
Fly 1/32nd Hawker Hurricane Mk IId
Kit No.: 32015   Material: IM, Pe, R
Manufacturer: Fly, Czech Republic
UK Price: £48.70

with the main gear bay being very well done but the rest of it fairly unremarkable, and even disappointing where the exhausts are concerned because they are not hollow cast, so I don't see much point to them myself. The etched parts are good with a very well done instrument panel, radiator bits and seat belts. There are also a number of tiny parts to add much later in the build, along with the levers for the cockpit. The instruction book offers 24 pages of construction steps (40 in total) as well as the excellent art for the four decal options on offer. All of the options are very good, with two desert, one SEAC and one Russian choice. The decals come on a single large sheet, including a comprehensive set of stencils, and they look very thin and beautifully printed.

Construction

This starts with the interior and it's all rather complicated due to the tubular construction of the real thing, with Fly making an accurate copy of it all. There are sixteen plastic parts, which need careful cleaning up, plus five resin bits, four little acetate sheets for the instrument dials and no fewer than 40 etched parts for most of the detailing. I would suggest taking the time to study the instructions and the parts in question to work out the best sequence for building it, as it really is a bit convoluted in there. My tip would be to leave out the control column and the connecting rods until after the main framework has been built because they really do get in the way beforehand. It's not easy to fit the completed thing into the fuselage either as there is a lot getting in the way. Plenty of patient trial fits and gentle trimming is the order of the day here. It's made infinitely easier by Fly because they moulded the framework is plastic and not cast resin, which makes it far more flexible and a much tougher sub-assembly to manhandle.

Construction of the main airframe sections is thankfully uneventful; just remember that trial fits and trims are a necessity as you go along. The main area of contention is the top of the undercarriage bay interfering with the fuselage and the wing sections. This means thinning out both the plastic and the resin parts to get them snuggled together. This makes lots of dust so remember to wear a mask.

The interior is neatly done, mostly in plastic but with a few little resin bits and the etched fret for the instrument panel and seat belts. It's a bit tricky to fit it into the fuselage, though

The resin wheel bay is nicely cast and fits well but there's a lot of work to be done in this area yet

The etched parts for the radiator matrix are very good but the bits to blank it off and stop it being see-through aren't mentioned in the instructions, and I didn't even know they were on the sprue until I had made one piece

The wings and tail fit reasonably well, although a bit of filler here and there won't go amiss, and the wings are helped with etched reinforcing bands for the joints' lower sections, covering them up very nicely.

The only part that needs some serious help is that big tropical air filter under the nose. It needs lots of filler around the front where it tries to match the contours of the engine cowling. It also needs the area just below the intake section reprofiled to make it look a little more 'pouty'. Sorry about that but I have no better way to describe it. The kit part is a constant arc from front to back whereas it should be flatter along the front. When you come to fit it you'll see what I mean.

I also fitted the undercarriage units before painting as well, mainly because I knew they were complex and didn't want to damage the paint in the process. They are indeed complex with a number of small actuators and links to fit and I guess they do fit but not in a particularly positive fashion. It's a bit vague getting everything into position but at least the plastic is

The light support structure is resin and delicate, while I replaced the crude kit light with a new clear bit. The etched support arm is neat, though

A lot to see here with the rocker cover bumps as separate items, the exhaust blanks, the very good centre line joint, and note that you have to take a lot of resin off the top of the wheel bay to get it all to fit

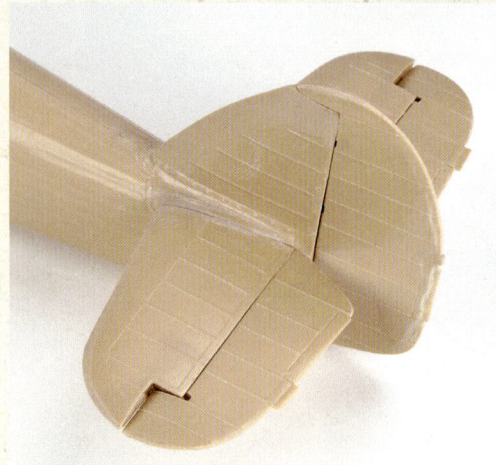

The tail pieces fit very nicely, with separate control surfaces and reasonable fabric effects

Once the busy underside is constructed it starts to look pretty good; that big air filter on the nose will take some blending in and reshaping, though

The undercarriage units are all plastic and quite a complicated set-up, so a lot of care is needed here, as well as some stretched sprue support arms, missing from the kit

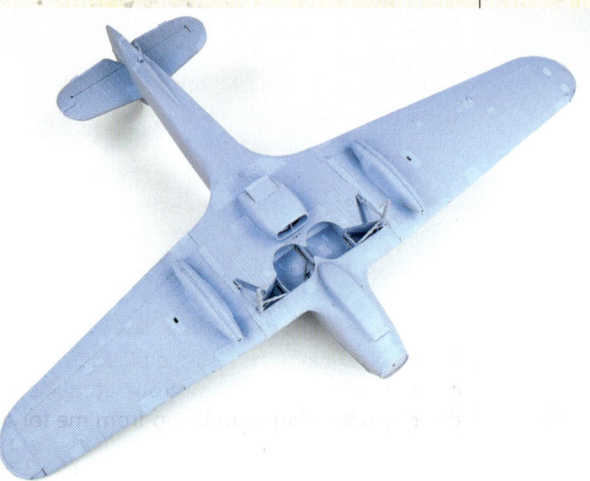

Azure Blue from White Ensign, with a few panels picked out in a lightened version. I went with the undercarriage bay in this colour as well, even though it could be Grey/Green or Aluminium

Upper surface Mid Stone from Humbrol, once again note the lightened panels

quite tough and resilient, allowing some leeway in adjustments.

Colour & Markings

And so to paint, the options in the box are all excellent, with the SEAC and Russian ones being immediately ignored for this project, which leaves two desert options, both No.6 Squadron 'The Flying Can Openers'. Both are in standard colours and patterns (A scheme, reverse colours I believe) with the classic Dark Earth/Middle Stone/Azure Blue set-up it's only the differences in markings that distinguish them. There are plenty of photographs of JV*Z and it looks to me as if it had the lighter Mediterranean Blue underside and not the Azure but that's a personal choice interpreting black and white images. While we are talking colours, please ignore the Humbrol numbers in the Fly painting guide as they are nothing like the ones you need.

I started with the White Ensign Azure Blue ACRN12 undersides, with highlighting and light shades for some of the panels. The upper surface followed after a bit of masking and the Mid Stone (Humbrol 93) is the base coat with 29 (Dark Earth), hand sprayed on top of that. Minimal masking for the camouflage pattern made it quick and easy, so after a night drying out the weathering was applied using my usual pastel dust and Tamiya Smoke methods. Various shades of the main colours were also used to give a very mottled and worn effect. The desert is harsh on paint and by the time these aircraft were replaced in 1943 they were pretty much worn out. As a side note, the Mk IId was replaced in North Africa by the rocket- and bomb-armed Mk IV before being transferred over to Italy to support the invasion there.

The paint was sealed in under a good coat of Tamiya X-22 Gloss Clear and it was on to the decals. As mentioned before, these decals look great on the sheet and in use they worked very well. They take a little bit of time to release from the backing paper and they have the awful habit of wrapping round themselves, especially the smaller ones, but they do look good once dry. They settle down with absolutely zero silvering

Dark Earth, Humbrol style, and a bit more shading with the lightened versions of the basic colours

Weathering is mostly pastel dust and done heavy handed as the pictures of this aircraft show it to be pretty rotten at the end of its service life

and after a quick brush of Microscale softening solution they conform perfectly, giving a very smooth surface. A little grey pastel dust to cut back the colour a little and another coat of gloss and we're ready for the final stages.

Final Details

There is a lot to do here, made worse by the multitude of etched parts waiting until the end and the fact that I had to do a serious bit of alteration as well. Basically the canopy, whilst it's nice and clear, is just too thick to be positioned open. I thinned down the framework on the inside as much as I dared but in the end had to take the grinders to the 'kennel' at the rear of the cockpit. This section of plywood fuselage just aft of the cockpit is at least nice and smooth, so sanding and reprofiling it wasn't too taxing. Obviously it messed up the paint and in hindsight I should have done it earlier in the build but, live and learn. The other major parts are the undercarriage doors, which need the brake lines attached and of course, the big, spear-pointed prop. The spinner looks very good, with the right shape and length but there are lots of blades in the box, so make sure you get the right ones. The gun barrels need slimming down and drilling out but they fit very well and of course there is then the multitude of delicate, easily breakable bits to do. Including the exhausts, which I have to admit I binned and used some Quickboost resin replacements, which are beautifully hollow cast.

The final finish was courtesy of Xtracolor XDFF flat vanish and the aerial wire is nothing more than 2lb fishing line and a bit of paint for the insulator at the tail. Job done.

Verdict

The Hurricane deserves all the plaudits it gets and it deserves all the attention from kit makers, so this one gets a big thumbs-up from me for all sorts of reasons. The fact that Fly have chosen to produce a whole raft of versions in this scale can only be a great thing and this kit is worth the effort to get something beautiful from it. The plastic is good, with excellent detail and although it is a little rougher than a Tamiya offering, that's

That's a lot of bits, not including the canopy and aerial wires. Check out the collection of tiny etched parts yet to be attached. Curse words are optional

no bad thing to do some honest-to-goodness 'modelling'. The resin is a bit of a disappointment (other than the gear bay) but the decals are very good, the instructions straightforward and the finished result has just the right 'look' to it. Considering I bought this with my own hard-earned cash, I wouldn't hesitate to get another.

Colours Used
Humbrol enamel:
29 Dark Earth
93 Desert Yellow (Mid Stone lookalike)
94 Brown Yellow
127 Ghost Grey
White Ensign Colourcoat enamel:
ACRN12 Azure Blue
Tamiya acrylic:
X-7 Red   X-19 Smoke
X-22 Gloss Clear
Xtracolor enamel:
XDFF Flat varnish

References

- Hawker Hurricane: Their history and how to model them by B. Robertson, G. Scarborough & R. Cross, Classic Aircraft No.4 (Patrick Stephens Ltd 1974 ISBN: 0-85059-124-4)
- Hawker Hurricane Described by F.K. Mason (Kookaburra Technical Publications 1970)
- Hawker Hurricane, Modellers' Datafile No.2 by R.A. Franks (SAM Publications, 1999 ISBN: 0-9533465-1-X)
- Hawker Hurricane by A. Juszczak & D. Karnas, Modelmania No.4 (AJ-Press 1999 ISBN: 83-7237-18-4)
- Hawker Hurricane cz.2 by D. Karlenko, R. Michulec & M. Rys, Monografie Lotnitzce No.52 (AJ-Press 2001 ISBN: 83-7237-084-2)
- Hawker Hurricane cz.3 by K. Janowicz, Monografie Lotnitzce No.53 (AJ-Press 2002 ISBN: 83-7237-094-X)
- Hawker Hurricane cz.4 by K. Janowicz, Monografie Lotnitzce No.54 (AJ-Press 2002 ISBN: 83-7237-095-8)
- Hawker Hurricane by P. Jacobs (The Crowood Press 1998 ISBN: 1-86126-12-8)
- Hawker Hurricane by Robert Jackson (Blandford Press 1988 ISBN: 0-7137-1683-5)
- Hawker Hurricane, Aero Detail No.12 (Dia Nippon Kaiga Co., Ltd, 1994 ISBN: 4-499-22636-8)
- Hawker Hurricane by Marek Rys, Yellow Series No.6122 (Mushroom Model Publications 2007 ISBN: 978-83-89450-32-1)
- Hawker Hurricane by E. Shacklady, Classic WWII Aviation Vol.1 (Tempus Publishing Ltd 2000 ISBN: 0-7524-2000-3)
- Hawker Hurricane by R. Gretzyngier & J. Ledwoch (Wydawnictwo Militaria 1999 ISBN: 83-7219-033-X)
- Hawker Hurricane – Inside and Out by M. Hiscock (The Crowood Press 2003 ISBN: 1-86126-630-8)
- Hurricane, Lock-On No.25 (Verlinden Publications, 1994)
- Hurricane, Walk Around No.15 by R. Mackay (Squadron/Signal Publications 1998 0-89747-388-4)

Historical Significance

The Hurricane is so well known that any stories about them have been told many times over, and even though the Battle of Britain may have been their finest moment, the sterling work they did later as fighter-bombers was no less important. Once Spitfire production took over and the Hurricane began to be replaced, new and equally exciting jobs came its way. One of those jobs was as a tank-buster, using massive cannons to overpower the armour of the new German Panzers. The basic Mk II airframe was updated with 40mm Vickers 'S' guns, one under each wing in a rather clumsy looking pod. The gun itself was strong and reliable in service, firing a tungsten tipped, 2½lb projectile out to ranges of 2,500 yards, capable of penetrating about 2in of armour. This was more than enough for the side and rear plating of the German tanks. Desert life is harsh for any aircraft but with a sensitive engine like the Merlin on board, the tropical filters and extra equipment to cope with the sand and grime was a must. Even though that filter attachment didn't do the looks any good, it helped to keep the grit out of the inner workings. With the addition of extra armour in later aircraft, as well as the drag of the pods and filter, these were amongst the slowest of all the Hurricanes. The squadrons loved the Hurricane because it was extremely tough, reliable and easy to fly, which is just what they needed for such low-level operations. And although losses were high the tank busters of No.6 Squadron did such a momentous job they were called 'The Flying Can Openers', a name that has stuck with them from that day to this.

Breda Ba 88 Lince, '11', 7° Gruppo, 5° Stormo RA, Castel Benito, Libya, 1940
Giallo Mimetico with Verde Mimetico mottling upper surfaces; Grigio Mimetico undersides.
White '11' on red pennant on nose. White undersides of wingtips

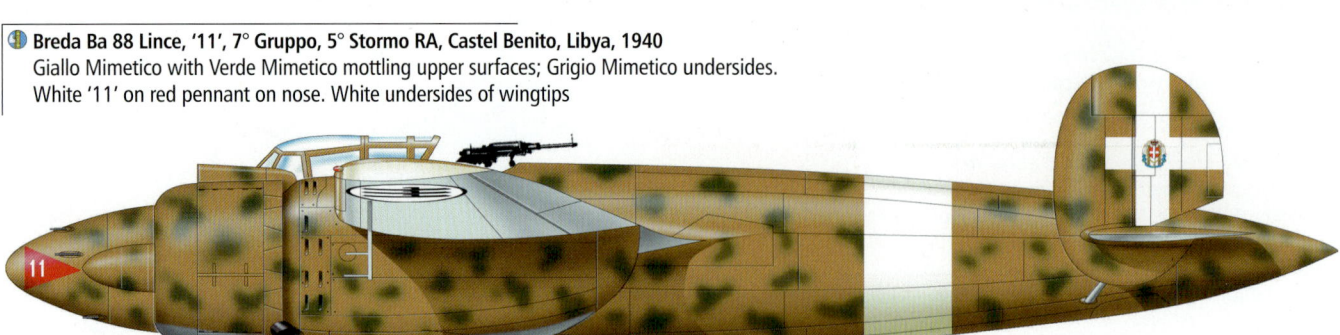

Breda Ba.65/A-80 Nibbio, 159-12, 159 ^ Squadriglia (12° Gruppo, 50° Stormo) RA, Libya, autumn 1940
Giallo/Verde Mimetico upper surfaces with Grigio Mimetico undersides; codes in black and red.
Unit badge on fin; name 'Antonio Dell'Oro' in gold below cockpit

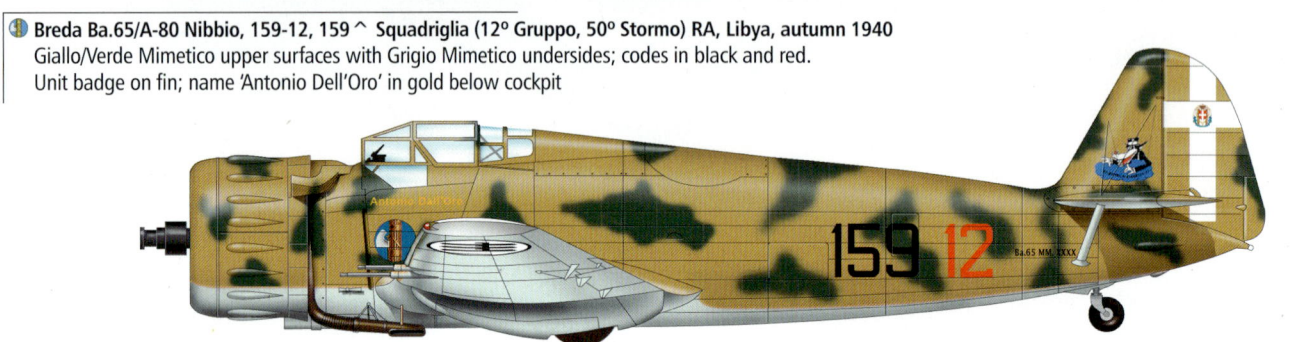

Fiat G.50bis Freccia, 359-3, 154° Gruppo Autonomon RA, Berat, early 1941, just before the move to Devoli on January 15
Giallo Mimetico 3 upper surfaces with mottles in Marrone Mimetico and Verde Mimetico 3; undersides in Grigio Mimetico.
Yellow engine cowl; hen in the marking faces forward, both sides

Caproni Ca.309 Ghibli, MM.11803/12-4, 12 ^ Squadriglia RA, Agedabia, July 1942
Giallo/Verde Mimetico upper surfaces with Grigio Mimetico undersides; white fuselage band with code in black and red.
White wingtips; black serial on fuselage sides below tailplane

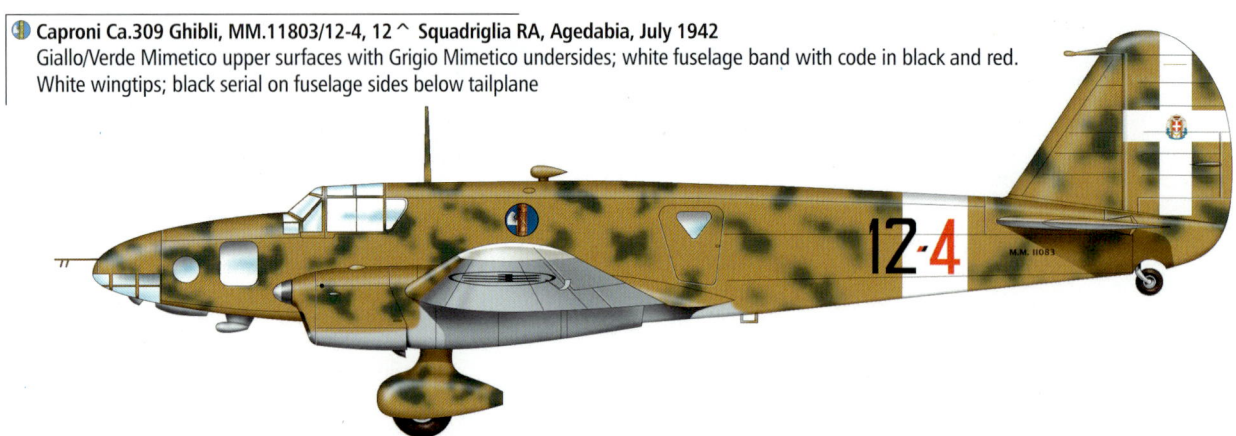

Caproni Ca.311, 32-4, 32 ^ Squadriglia, 15° Gruppo Osservazione Aerea RA, Libya, 1941
Giallo/Verde Mimetico upper surfaces with Grigio Mimetico undersides; white fuselage
band with code in black/red. 'Scorpion' badge in black on fin

Fiat CR.42 Falco Serie XIII, 20-10 of 20^ Squadriglia, 156° Gruppo, 15° Stormo d'Assalto RA, Libya 1941
Verde Oliva Scuro 2 with large mottles in Nocciola Chiaro 4 upper surfaces; Grigio Azzurro Chiaro 1 undersides.
White rear fuselage band and '20' of code, red spinner and '10' of code. Serial and stencil data in red.
Note underwing bombs

Fiat CR.42 Falco, 412-2, flown by Ten. Mario Visentini, 412^ Squadriglia Autonoma RA, Gura, summer 1940
Giallo/Verde Mimetico upper surfaces with Grigio Mimetico undersides; silver spinner. Code in black/red;
personal marking on rear fuselage sides. National markings in black with white background above
and below wings

**Macchi MC.202 Folgore Serie III, M.M.7720/84-1, flown by Serg. Piero Buttazzi, 84^ Squadriglia,
10° Gruppo, 4° Stormo RA, Fuka (Egypt), September 1942**
Nocciola Chiaro 4 upper surfaces with irregular bands of Verde Oliva Scuro 2; note different pattern on rear upper engine
cowling panel. Starboard wing comes from a different aircraft finished with 'smoke ring' pattern. White spinner,
wingtips and rear fuselage band; codes in black and red. '4° F.Baracca' signature on nose,
unit badge on fuselage band; no House of Savoy badge on rudder cross.
This aircraft was also flown by fighter ace Cap. Franco Lucchini

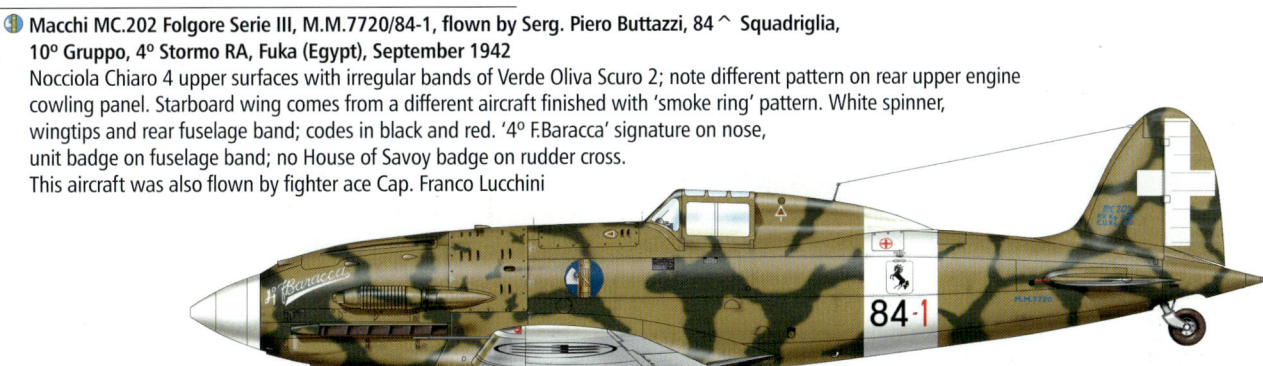

**Macchi MC.202 Folgore Serie IX, M.M.9400/88-9, flown by Mar.llo Gianino Baschirotto, 88^ Squadriglia,
6° Gruppo, 1° Stormo RA, Gabes (Tunisia), spring 1943**
Nocciola Chiaro 4 upper surfaces with Verde Oliva Scuro 2 'smoke rings'
Grigio Azzurro Chiaro1 undersides; white spinner and rear fuselage band.
Codes in black and red, with white drop shadow;
unit badge on fuselage band

Macchi MC.202 Folgore Serie II, M.M.7844/91-3, 91^ Squadriglia, 10° Gruppo, 4° Stormo, Libya, 1942
One of only 30 examples in the new 'desert' scheme of Nocciola Chiaro 4/Verde Oliva Scuro 2 to be issue by Macchi in
'reversed' colours; Grigio Azzurro Chiaro 1 undersides. White spinner front,
rear fuselage band and underside of wingtips; codes in black/red.
Unit badge on fuselage band; note unpainted sand filter

🔵 **Macchi MC.200 Saetta, '365-1', 365^ Squadriglia, 150° Gruppo Autonomo RA, En Nofilia, Libya, January 1942**
Nocciola Chiaro and Verde Oliva Scuro upper surfaces with Grigio Azzurro Chiaro undersides;
white fuselage band and cross on vertical tail surfaces.
Codes in white and red

🔵 **Macchi MC.200 Saetta, 85-4, flown by Ten. Giuseppe Re, 85^ Squadriglia, 18° Gruppo, 3° Stormo RA, North Africa, September 1942**
Nocciola Chiaro upper surfaces with Verde Oliva Scuro mottles; Grigio Azzurro Chiaro undersides. '85' in black, with white drop
shadow on fuselage sides aft of white band; '4' on fin in red,
with white drop shadow. Unit badge on white band

🔵 **IMAM Ro.37bis Lince, MM.10789, 115^ Squadriglia Osservazione Aerea RA (Aerial Reconnaissance), North Africa, October 1940**
Giallo Mimetico with Verde Mimetico mottles on upper surfaces;
Grigio Mimetico on undersides. Codes in black

🔵 **IMAM Ro.63, 132-1, 132^ Squadriglia Osservazione Aerea RA, Libya, 1941**
Giallo/Verde/Marrone Mimetico upper surfaces with Grigio Mimetico undersides;
white rear fuselage band. Code in black/red; rank pennant aft on mid-fuselage

🔵 **Savoia-Marchetti SM.74, '2' (ex-I-ALPE), 616a^ Squadriglia (154° Gruppo) RA, Libya, 1940**
Giallo/Verde/Marrone Mimetico upper surfaces with Grigio Mimetico undersides; black/white markings above
and below wings. Code '2' in red; note nose marking outlined in white

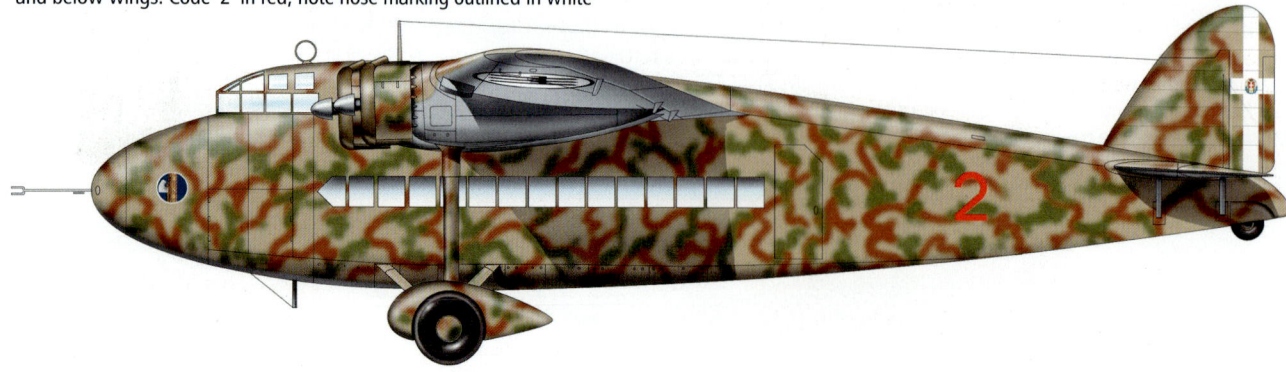

Savoia-Marchetti SM.79 Sparviero, 18-1, 18 ^ Squadriglia, 27º Gruppo, 8º Stormo RA, Castelbenito, summer 1941
Verde Mimetico 1/Giallo Mimetico 1/Marrone Mimetico irregular band camouflage on upper surfaces; Grigio Azzurro Chiaro undersides. Giallo Cromo engine cowlings; codes in black/red. Type 2 markings above and below wings

Savoia-Marchetti SM.79 Sparviero, MM.21434, 284 ^ Squadriglia Autonoma Aerosilurante RA, Benghazi, early 1942
Giallo Mimetico 1 upper surfaces with large patches in Verde Mimetico 1 and 2; Grigio Azzurro Chiaro undersides.
Code in black/red; spinners white

Savoia-Marchetti SM.81 Pippistrello, 218 ^ Squadriglia (54° Gruppo, 16° Stormo) RA, Libya, March 1941
Giallo Mimetico 3 and Verde Mimetico 3 upper surfaces with Grigio Mimetico undersides. White fuselage band.
Codes in black and red.
Unit badge on fin

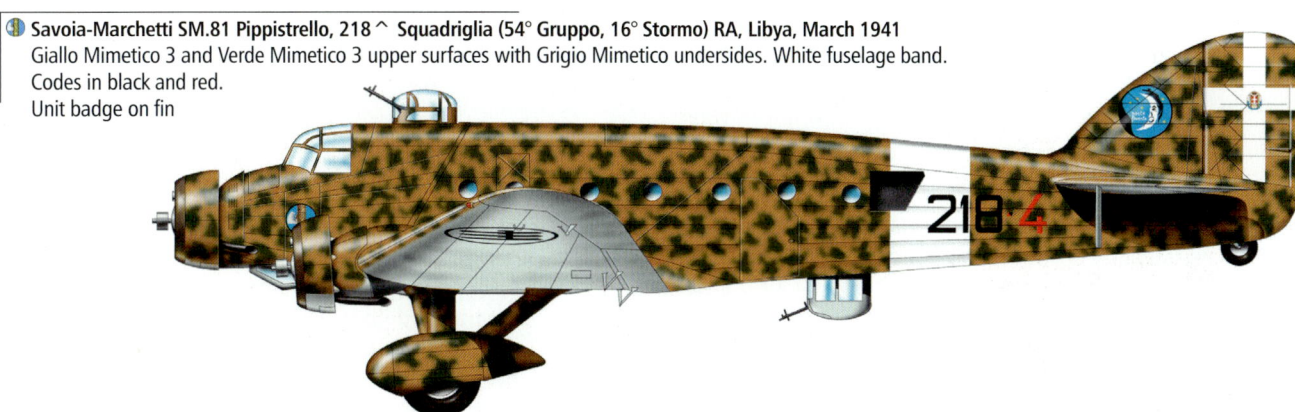

Savoia-Marchetti SM.82 Marsupiale, 610-9, 610 ^ Squadriglia RA, North Africa, 1942
Giallo Mimetico 3 upper surfaces with Verde Mimetico 3 and Marrone Mimetico mottling; Grigio Azzurro Chiaro undersides. White rear fuselage band; wing fasces markings in black with white background. Unit code in black and red

Junkers Ju 87R-2 Picchiatello, 209-8, 209 ^ Squadriglia, 97º Gruppo Autonomo Bombardamento a Tuffo RA, Derna (Libya), summer 1941
RLM 70/71/65 with previous German markings overpainted in Verde Mimetico on upper surfaces and Grigio Mimetico on undersides; Giallo Cromo band around engine cowling, '8' on wheel spats and '209' on fuselage. White band around rear fuselage and cross on tail

Heinkel He 111H-6

1/72nd

by Libor Jekl

The new-tool He 111 kit from Hasegawa was first produced in 2004 and this particular kit was released a year later. In the intervening years they have progressively released several different boxings of the H and P versions, while the H-6 has also been released under the Revell label. The kit consists of sixteen sprues giving a total of about 140 parts, of which 22 are clear, all done in Hasegawa's usual 'multi-purpose' tooling to offer all the various alternative parts via numerous sprues. Hasegawa did not cover the very late H versions because these differed substantially (powered dorsal turret, modified cockpit glazing and belly gondola, etc.), any potential fit issues are limited to the separately moulded engine cowlings (because of the Daimler Benz engines of the P versions) and the armament variations coupled with their appropriate gun positions and alternative cupolas, none of which complicate the build at all. All the parts are extremely cleanly moulded in their usual grey-coloured (harder) plastic with sharply defined and fine panel lines. The transparencies are crystal clear and thin without a single blemish, and they also seem to be cleverly split from the construction point of view. The cockpit interior looks well detailed, as are the upper gun position, bomb bay and overall details for the landing gear. The example I used included two LT F5b torpedoes with their PVC 1006B racks however, these were not needed and so were kept for a future project. The late H-6 version I intended to build used the Junkers VS-11 wooden propeller with a larger spinner, which had to be sourced elsewhere because the kit provides only the narrow VDM units (the VS-11 propellers are included in the He 111Z kit). Also, I did not use the kit's decal sheet, which offers markings for three KG26 machines operating in 1941 from Sicily, but opted for a V./KG100 machine based in Autumn 1942 at Kalamaki on Zakynthosin island instead, this being one of the most colourful options of the Xtradecal sheet X72248.

Construction

With this particular type it's best to assemble the airframe first and add the cockpit along with its transparencies at the end, in order to

The Hasegawa kit box

Technical Data
Hasegawa 1/72nd Heinkel He 111H-6 'with torpedo'
Kit No.: 00753   Material: IM
Manufacturer: Hasegawa, Japan
UK Price: £OOP

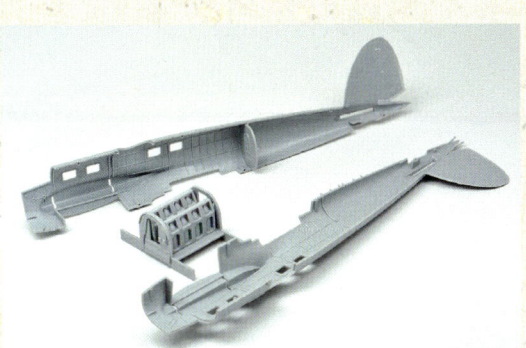

The interior detail in the kit is good and includes such things as the vertical bomb cells

As little or none of the interior would be visible once the model was built, no extra detailing was undertaken and the fuselage halves were quickly joined together

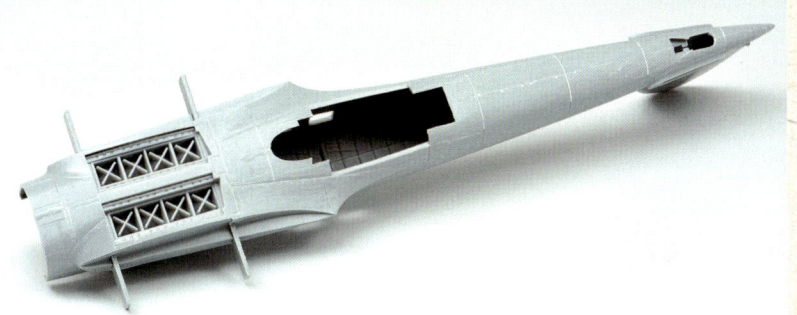

The interior needs to be painted a suitable shade, as a lot will be visible up through the glazed ventral gondola

The wheel wells inserts are very bare in the kit, so the photo-etched panels from the Eduard exterior detail set were used to liven the areas up, as well as box off the rear region, which is otherwise depicted open in the kit

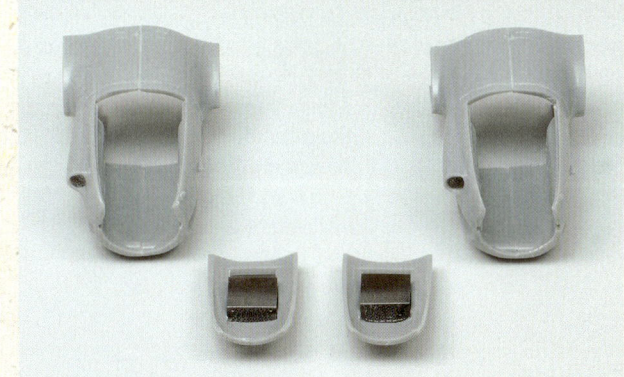

Photo-etched parts were used in the carburettor intakes and ventral radiators of each engine unit

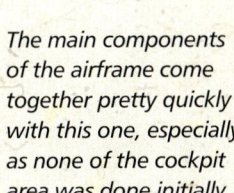

The main components of the airframe come together pretty quickly with this one, especially as none of the cockpit area was done initially

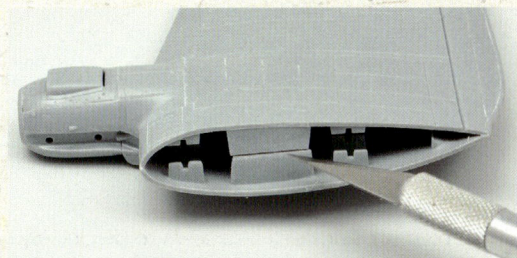

Don't join together the tabs moulded inside the wing roots, as this will cause the wing cross-section to no longer match the corresponding area at the fuselage/root area

Very little filler or sanding was necessary for the main airframe, everything was then polished with sanding pads and special cloths from Gunze-Sangyo

The underside did not need much in the way of filler either

The edges of the fuselage windows were brush-painted with black, so the light-coloured plastic was not visible through the clear plastic panels once installed

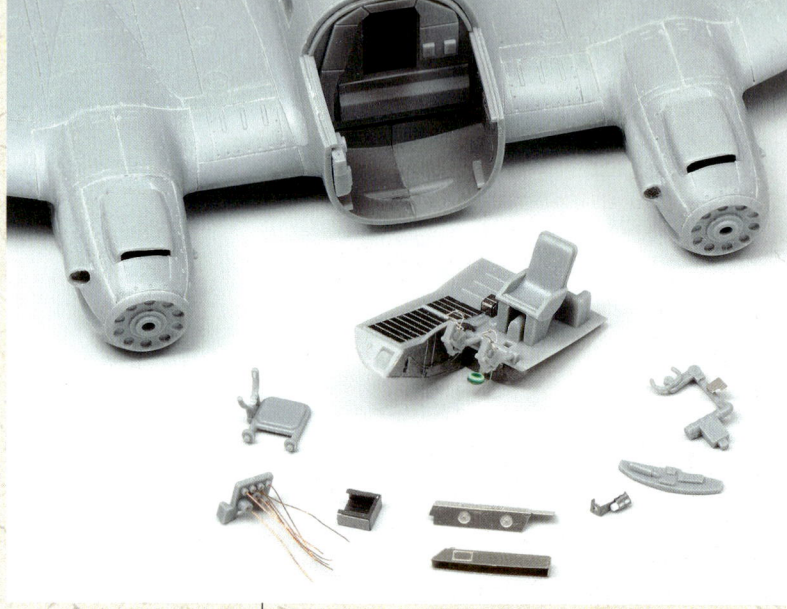

The inboard sections of the machine-guns were attached to the clear panels before they were installed; the barrels and sights would be added once all assemble and painting was completed

The cockpit interior combines the kit parts with photo-etched details from the Eduard interior detail set, plus some lengths of copper wire

The pre-painted instrument panel looked more like RLM 02 than RLM 66, so very dilute layers of RLM 66 (H416) were sprayed on until the colour looked better

The interior assembled and painted with the pre-painted belts looking very effective

avoid potential damage to the fragile cockpit detail, as well as reducing the risk of dust getting inside. I therefore commenced the build with the assembly of the individual bomb cells along with the fuselage bulkheads that were moulded integrally with the half spars that ensure the correct position of the wing halves. The bomb bay looks pretty nice, having moulded into it the bomb bodies with their tail stabilisers visible at the bottom, however, I planned to close the bay so I did not bother with any additional detailing here or in the rear fuselage because none of it would be visible. The bomb bay was painted H416 RLM 66, inserted inside and the fuselage halves were then cemented together. The bay was then closed with the separately moulded one-piece doors, which required some sanding to fit properly. From the rear fuselage underside I removed the antenna mountings because it would hinder cleaning up the seam line at that point. I would later drill new holes then add a new antenna made from stretched sprue. From the rear cone I also cut off the barrel of the fixed machine-gun, as this was often removed in the field and it seemed to be omitted from the machine I was depicting.

I continued with the wheel bays and these were partially replaced with etched parts from Eduard's exterior detail set (#72436) because these offered finer rib details and featured sidewall detail plus some brackets inside as well as plugs for the rear bay parts which are otherwise left open in the kit. Next the cowlings were glued together, each consisting of four parts and fortunately these all matched very well and needed only a few drops of cyanoacrylate to level minor imperfections in the joints. From the etched I used the radiator faces and the nacelles could then be inserted into the assembled wing halves. Once again the fit was more than satisfactory and the joints were only sanded smooth with fine wet and dry, then any damaged panel lines rescribed with fine razor saw and polished. I do not recommend that you glue together the vertical tabs moulded inside the wing halves that determine the wing root height, because on one side I had to cut the joint through and release

The repainted instrument and overhead consoles were carefully attached to the upper section of the nose glazing

it otherwise the wing height did not match the height at the corresponding fuselage aperture. Trial assembly of things like the tailplanes showed no major fit issues, though, so the parts were cemented together. I cleaned up the joints with sanding sticks and removed any dust residues with Mr Grinding Cloths and a toothbrush. Only on the underside of the wing/fuselage region did I need to fill some joint lines with Mr White Putty, immediately removing any excess with a cotton bud soaked in cyanoacrylate debonder. I continued with the installation of the side windows, the first couple of which was covered with metal sheet on the real aircraft. The rear window openings had their edges brush-painted with black to avoid any light-coloured plastic showing through and before the clear panels were installed, I attached the inner parts of the MG 17 machine guns because their barrels were left off until the end of the build. The clear parts were then fixed in place using Gator Grip PVA.

Now I could deal with the cockpit details, which were a combination of kit parts and etched from the Eduard interior detail set (#73247). Unfortunately Eduard painted the etched in a colour that looks more like RLM 02, however the interior would have been RLM 66 for a machine of the era I was depicting. Because I did not want to sand the etched parts back to bare metal and I also wanted to keep the great printed details on the dials and instrument faces, I carefully tried to overspray the affected parts with a heavily diluted coat of H416 RLM 66, which eventually looked more appropriate. Once all the interior parts and extra details were

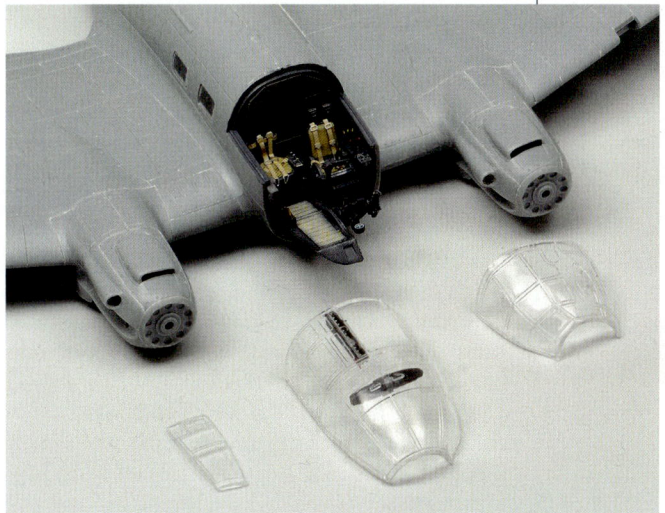

The three main sections of the nose glazing, less the front cupola

The clear parts all fitted without problem, the sliding hatch is left off until the final assembly stage

fixed in situ I could add the canopy, which is split into five parts and that initially caused me some concern. A couple of dry-fitting sessions quickly showed that the fit was just fine between the clear parts themselves and with the fuselage cross section. The parts were therefore fixed step by step with a minute amount of extra thin glue. I started with the bottom part then added the side window and at the same time I added the upper part without applying glue so that once all was adjusted to my satisfaction I fixed it in situ. The upper sliding hood was left off until a later stage, as was the nose cupola. I continued with the ventral gondola where again all matched nicely with the corresponding opening in the fuselage. Some care was needed with the selection of the correct gun positions though and in my case I used the front one with the MG-FF cannon (#T1), and the three small windows in the gondola centre underside had to be filled or just painted over because these were not present on a late H-6. Into the clear parts I cemented the inner sections of the guns, as once again the barrels would be added at the end of construction and painting. The only remaining parts now were the radiators, which received etched screens and the bodies were then cemented into the wing. The rear flaps looked a bit thick so the replacement etched components saved the day here. I masked off all the transparencies with the Eduard masks (#CX003), which I consider mandatory here due to the large glazed areas of the type, combined with pieces of foam to seal any remaining openings in the fuselage. The whole thing was now primed with Mr Surfacer 1000 (grey), while the canopy frames were coated with Mr Finishing Surfacer 1500 (black) to ensure the following paint layers had a solid base.

Colour & Markings

The machine (6N+DG) I was depicting wore on the upper surfaces the usual Luftwaffe bomber splinter scheme of RLM 70 and RLM 71, however this scheme was locally modified with large irregular RLM 79 patches bordered with thinner RLM 80 bands. The RLM 65 undersurfaces were oversprayed in black since KG100's aircraft were intended for night attacks. I started off my painting session with the underside, but I opted for H77 Tyre Black for the base coat instead of pure black just to add a better tonal (scale) effect, and

The Eduard pre-cut masking set is a must with something like the He 111 due to the extensive glazed nose area

The radiator screens were from the Eduard photo-etched detail set, the rear flaps in the covers can be seen removed in the background and these too would also be replaced with etched parts

The inner sections of the machine-gun and cannon in the ventral position have to be painted and attached inside the clear sections before they are glued in position

the surface was then gently post-shaded along the panel lines with H12 Black and H313 Yellow. The splinter scheme on the upper surfaces was applied freehand using H64 RLM 71 and H65 RLM 70 without much care paid to the exact shape of the individual areas because most of them would be over-sprayed in the next step. The RLM 79 was mixed from H79 Sand Yellow and H310 Brown in a 50:50 ratio with a drop of H327 Red that added a slightly pinkish hue to it. Again I did not have to pay much attention to the precise shape of the RLM 79 patches because apparently the single preserved photo of this machine

shows only the left side, so this explains why the panting guide in the Xtradecal instructions do not show the other side. I checked a number of known photos of KG100 machines from this period so I can call my version an 'educated guess'. The RLM 79 areas were bordered with H420 RLM 80, then I dealt with any overspray and the surface was fixed with few thin coats of GX100 Super Clear III.

Now I could apply the decals, which are printed to Xtradecal's high standards. However they can sometimes react excessively to certain decal solutions, don't panic, they always bed down again nicely without any adverse effects left on the surface. Based on my research I believe this aircraft wore the individual code letter 'D' on the wing leading edges, which can be seen in photos of 6N+AG from the same unit after it made a belly landing, so I sourced suitable letters from my decal bank. The lower wing Balkenkreuz would be blackened out due to night operations, so the white portions of it were subtly oversprayed with a black mixture. As can be observed on period photos the exhaust stains were usually quite heavy on the He 111, wrapping around the leading edges and spreading along a broad portion of the wing, so these were airbrushed

The clear sections are primed with black, whilst the remainder of the airframe is done with grey

Pure black is too intense for scale work, so in this instance the 'black' undersides were reproduced with Tyre Black

Once the black undersides were on, the panel lines were high and low-lighted with pure black and yellow

The standard splinter pattern of RLM 70 and 71 was applied freehand to the upper surfaces, so precise sharp edges were not needed due to the RLM 79 that was going to be applied over the top

The field-applied RLM 79 went on next, again applied freehand

The final colour was some RLM 80 to border the RLM 79 regions

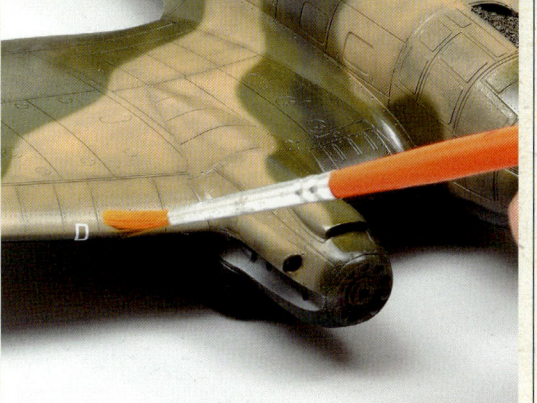

Additional 'Ds' in white were needed on the leading edge of each outer wing panel and these came from the spares box, as none are supplied on the Xtradecals sheet

The VS 11 propellers and spinners came from the Quickboost range, as the kit only includes the VDM units

Wires and brake lines were added to the undercarriage legs, then the wheels were replaced with ones from Aires simply because the kit parts are split vertically, which leads to a seam line across the tyre tread

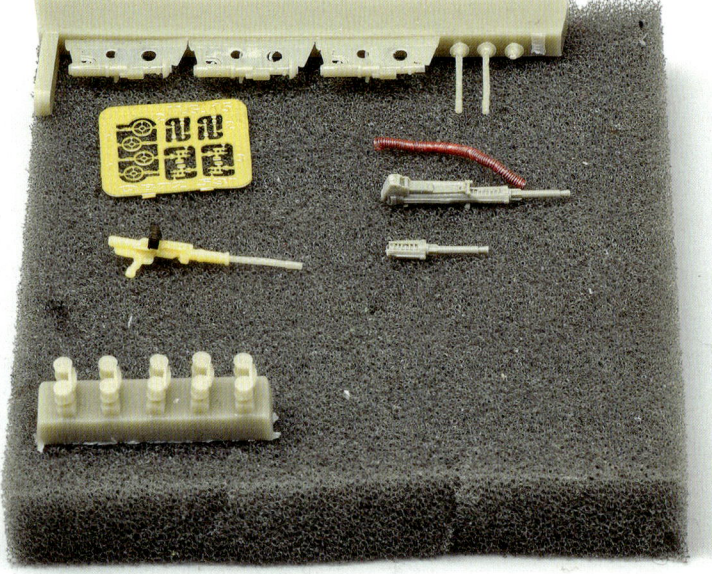

The machine-gun and cannon for the nose and dorsal turret were all sourced from old Aires sets, the spent cartridge case chute being made from thin wire wrapped about a larger piece

The crosses on the undersides of the wings were toned down with a heavily diluted layer of black

The dorsal turret painted and assembled prior to being slotted into the fuselage and its upper cover added

The nose cupola with the MG-FF cannon installed prior to attachment to the nose glazing

Exhaust staining is heavy on the He 111, so this was applied freehand with an airbrush using dilute black and grey

Weathering and rust on the exhaust stacks was done via crushed artists' chalks

on using a thin mixture of black and a light grey. The exhausts were then picked out in black and brown colours using powder ground from a set of artistic chalks.

Final Details

The VS-11 propellers were eventually sourced from the Quickboost set intended for the Hasegawa Ju 88G kit (#QB72190), which were almost identical, all I had to do was sand the propeller tips to a more gentle shape. The landing gear components received some photo-etched cables and braces and were ready to be mounted in the wheel bays. I did not follow the instruction suggestions and installed them progressively because that allowed better alignment inside and resulted in a sturdy unit. The wheels were eventually replaced with Aires resin items (#7126) that offered subtle hub and tread pattern detail and also saves some time because the kit parts were split in two halves. The various weapons and barrels were sourced out of my spares box, being mostly leftovers from older Aires sets, while the nose MG-FF cannon spent-cartridges chute was scratchbuilt from 1.5mm thick lead wire wrapped with a thin copper wire. All parts were primed with Mr Finishing Surfacer 1500 (Black) and polished to a metal sheen with MIG Production's Gun Metal pigment. The MG 17 for the upper position was glued inside the turret, which could be assembled and painted separately and inserted inside, then it was covered with its hood. In the nose cupola I installed the MG-FF cannon with some wiring added from copper wire and the part was carefully fixed on the cockpit glazing using a small amount of cyanoacrylate. Now I added etched details such as the gunsights, the antenna mast supports and fixed the aerial on it cut from Uschi van den Rosten 'Fine' elastic rigging thread – job done!

Verdict

The He-111H from Hasegawa is a quality kit that unlike other kits from this manufacturer offers a detailed interior including the bomb bay (their newer kits all tended to be a little 'sparse' as far as moulded/supplied interior detail goes), plus sharp surface detail and panel lines. However, as with any He 111 kit the focal point here is the large cockpit 'greenhouse' and it's here that Hasegawa clearly win with their perfect rendition

of these parts that do not make the assembly overly complex. At the moment we have the recent new kit from Airfix to consider, which seems to offer comparable, if not better detailed in certain areas, so I leave the final judgement to the personal tastes and preferences of individual modellers. The real weak point of this manufacturer's products was their restricted and limited availability, but if you have got the opportunity to obtain this kit for a favourable price or have the cheaper Revell reissue of it, do not be hesitant, as you will not be disappointed with it.

Paints Used	
Gunze-Sangyo Mr Color lacquer: GX100 Super Clear Gloss	
Gunze-Sangyo Mr Aqueous Color acrylic:	
H12 Black	H64 RLM 71
H65 RLM 70	H79 Sand Yellow
H310 Brown	H313 Yellow
H327 Red	H416 RLM 66
H420 RLM 80	
Gunze-Sangyo Mr Finishing Surfacer 1500 (Black)	
Gunze-Sangyo Mr Surfacer 1000 (Grey)	

References
- Heinkel He 111, Aero Detail No.18 (Dia Nippon Kaiga Co., Ltd 1997 ISBN: 4-499-22670-8)
- Heinkel He 111 – A Documentary History by H.J. Nowarra (Jane's Publishing Co., Ltd 1980 ISBN: 0-7106-0046-1)
- Heinkel He 111: Vom Original zum Modell by K.H. Regnat (Bernard & Graefe Verlag 2000 ISBN: 3-7637-6022-9)
- Heinkel He 111 by R. Michulec, Aircraft Monograph No.2 (AJ-Press 1994 ISBN: 83-86208-07-4)
- Heinkel He 111 – Part 1: The early variants A-G and J of the standard bomber aircraft of the Luftwaffe in WWII by M. Griehl. WWII Combat Aircraft Photo Archive No.4 (AirDOC 2006 ISBN: 3-935687-43-5)
- Heinkel He 111 Vol. I by K. Janowicz, Monograph No.3 (Kagero 2004 ISBN: 83-89088-26-6)
- Heinkel He 111 Vol. II by K. Janowicz, Monograph No.8 (Kagero 2005)

Historical Significance

Nazi Germany didn't need long-range bombers, or so they believed and because of that they stuck with twin-engined medium-range bomber designs throughout much of WWII. Because of this they had a number of fine designs that were used from the first days, right up until the final armistice in 1945. One of these ubiquitous machines was Heinkel's He 111 that came to be used just about everywhere and for any kind of mission they needed. During the North African campaign the Heinkel was initially used to bolster the flagging Italian operations but later came under the full control of the Luftwaffe. It carried out its usual jack-of-all-trades jobs, with reconnaissance, patrol and bombing missions being the primary tasks. Long-range strikes out into the Mediterranean and trying to keep Malta isolated were all part of the plan but the worsening situation on the African mainland meant that more and more time was spent attempting to blunt the British counter-attacks. Losses were high on these missions, not only due to the Allied fighters and anti-aircraft fire but also the harsh conditions under which the aircraft operated. Long ranges over featureless deserts kept the crews on constant edge and the failure of the supply ships bringing spare parts and fuel to the airfields made an impossible job for air and ground crews alike. Despite the difficulties, the He 111 was well liked by its crews because it was tough and reliable and loved by the ground crews because it was easy to work on and that big wing made for a lovely sunshade! Re-engined and refined, it remained in service after WWII with the Spanish, with the last of the German-built machines being retired in 1958 and as the CASA 2.111 it actually stayed operational until 1972!

Dewoitone D.520

1/72nd

by Libor Jekl

The RS Models kit box art

The RS Models company focuses in 1/72nd scale on less frequent aircraft types so it is not surprising that they covered this long-time neglected subject a few years ago. The only suitable choice in this scale, the Hasegawa kit first appeared over 20 years ago and it seems to be pretty long in the tooth nowadays. This new kit consists of 40 parts all on a single sprue plus a one-piece canopy and side windows, all done in the usual short-run fashion having no location pins and thick sprue gates. The plastic parts are cleanly moulded and that is especially apparent on the fuselage halves and wing, where no sign of flash or other imperfections can be found, the surface being completely smooth. The thin panel lines are consistent and sharp, it is just on some of the smaller parts that you will have to do some rescribing. These smaller parts also slightly suffer from the limitations of the moulding technology because the mould separation line is distinct and could do with some clean-up, mainly on the landing gear legs. The clear parts are nice and transparent and moulded without distortion, albeit they are little bit on the thick side. The cockpit looks quite busy and consists of the floor with the centre opening for the control column, rudder pedals, front and rear bulkheads, pilot's seat, gunsight along with its supporting console and the instrument panel with subtly raised instrument faces; plus the sidewalls feature some raised instruments and ribs as well. All looks convincing and usable considering the closed canopy option provided in the box; in comparison with the Hasegawa kit this is a huge improvement as its cockpit looked very simplified. A good amount of detail is also provided in the wheel wells and that was again a weak point of the Hasegawa kit. The landing gear itself is not bad either, although the wheel hubs lack the typical oval-shaped apertures on the hub's periphery. The instructions are printed on a single folded A4 sheet and they are supplemented with a colour sheet with the camouflage schemes that is shared with the other boxing covering the Free French machines. For more experienced modellers the instructions are a sufficient guide to start the work, however I believe less skilled modellers would need to examine the exact position of certain airframe elements such as the antenna, and the inclusion of a front-view depicting the right angle of the landing gear along with the wheels' slant would be very useful as well. The kit provides two spinners without giving further details, as a base guide though you can use the larger spinner with Ratier propeller for any aircraft up to serial number 350. The late (short) type of

Technical Data

RS Models 1/72nd Dewoitine D.520
Kit No.: 92101   Material: IM
Manufacturer: RS Models, Czech Republic
UK Price: £14.99

The interior detail is sufficient from the box, but Libor opted to add the photo-etched detail set from Brengun

The seat cushions and belts were picked out in more appropriate 'fabric' colours

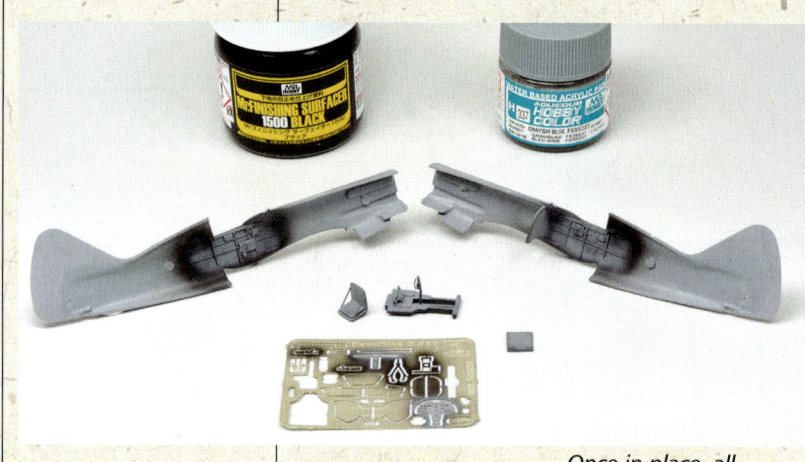

Once in place, all the interior parts were primed with Mr Finishing Surfacer 1500 (black), then with H337 greyish-blue

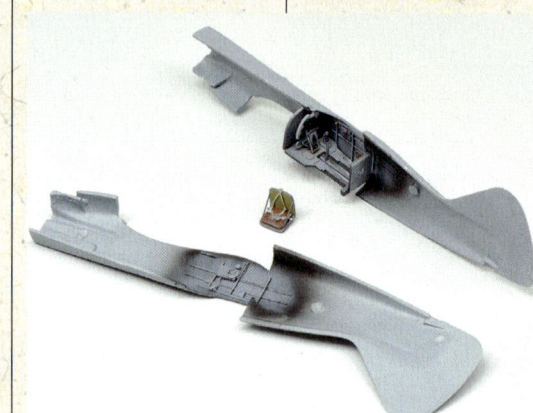

You will have to remove the prominent ejector pin mark from inside the ventral radiator unit using a rotary tool

The landing flaps were carefully cut from the wing halves with a razor saw

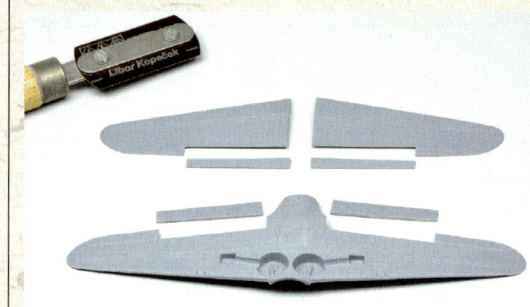

The bulkhead behind the pilot's head was scratchbuilt from plasticard to hide the vertical joint in this region

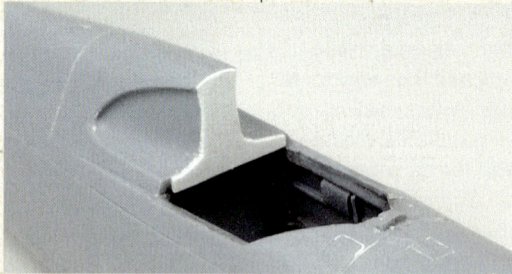

You need to remove a little plastic from the inner root edges of each wing half for it to fit snugly with the corresponding area of the fuselage

Once the wings are in place, you have to deal with a slight gap at the front with a plastic shim, whilst the rear joint has a small hole that can easily be filled with cyanoacrylate

spinner was used with the Chauvière propeller, however the kit provides only a single propeller with a somehow 'universal' shape. In fact there wasn't a great deal of difference between these two types (both were 3m diameter), so overall I think this is not a big issue.

Construction

I started the build with the preparation of the cockpit parts, which were first removed from the sprue and cleaned up. From the fuselage sidewalls I removed any ejector pin parks that might disturb later assembly, albeit these were not visible through the canopy/side window openings. Despite the fact that the cockpit is pretty reasonably detailed I wanted to go further, therefore I obtained the Brengun photo-etched detail set (#BRL72020), which furnished the seat belts, a more accurate instrument panel and the typical 'lantern' style OPL RX39 gunsight, among other parts. The assembled cockpit was therefore primed with Mr Finishing Surfacer 1500 (black) and airbrushed in a darker blue-grey shade (H337 Greyish Blue). Subsequently the fuselage halves could be joined using extra thin Mr Cement S without much trouble despite the lack of any locating pins; just the ventral air inlet on the nose needed a drop of cyanoacrylate to fill a little sink mark in it. Next I attached the sepa-

rately moulded nose with the air inlets to the oil coolers, which required a few strokes with a fine round file in order to give their walls appropriate scale thickness. The nose air intake with screen mesh can be easily damaged with excessive cement, so you may need to restore the individual subtle louvres with the fine edge of a razor saw, as I did.

Next I continued with the preparation of the wing halves; using a razor saw I removed the landing flaps and reduced the wall thickness at their hinge line with sanding sticks as well as the wing trailing edges, which were moulded slightly too thick. The assembled wing was trial fitted to the fuselage and this resulted in the need to remove about 1mm of plastic from both wing upper halves to ensure a reasonable fit. At the ventral joint line I filled the resulting tiny gap, despite it being barely apparent, as it does not seem to be present on the actual airframe, and the joint was further levelled with a layer of Mr Surfacer 500 and polished. Now I cemented in situ the extended landing flaps, which came from an older resin set by the French company Hi-Tech that was designed for the Hasegawa kit, but they matched the RS kit with a little adjustment. The flap hinges were scratchbuilt from 1mm circles

Mr Surfacer 500 applied with a brush, will level out the ventral wing joints at the leading and trailing edges

The landing flaps were replaced with those produced back in the 1990s for the Hasegawa kit; these resin parts need just a little modification to fit

The hinges for the landing flaps are reproduced with discs cut in plasticcard, that are then folded in half

punched from thin 0.2mm plastic sheet and cut into halves. The subtly raised panels overlapping the wing leading edge and over the machine gun apertures were accentuated with thin self-adhesive foil wrapped around the edge and trimmed to shape with a scalpel blade. Next I prepared the radiator bath, grinding off first a prominent ejector pin mark from its interior, and added the photo-etched radiator faces from the Brengun set along with the extended outlet flap.

I continued with the canopy which was replaced with the Falcon vacformed item (Clear-Vax Canopy Set No.26), while the side windows were used out of the box and I need to point out that they perfectly matched the openings, which helped to eliminate the possibility of marking them with cement when they were installed. Obviously, before that I painted the areas beneath with the interior colour. In the cockpit I installed the etched gunsight and fixed the windshield to the fuselage with a minute amount of cyanoacrylate. The transparencies were next masked off with a combination of Tamiya tape and Maskol, along with a few strips cut from flexible electrician's tape that allowed me to copy the curvatures on the front glass. The kit's surface was then primed with Mr Surfacer 1000 (grey), riveted according to a set of scale drawings, and using the Hasegawa scribing needle I restored any damaged fasteners on the cowling.

Colour & Markings

The aircraft operating with Armée de l'Air de Vichy wore the famous red and yellow identification stripes that make them truly unmistakable. However, their application does not seem to follow strict rules and their size and location may vary between individual D.520s, even those

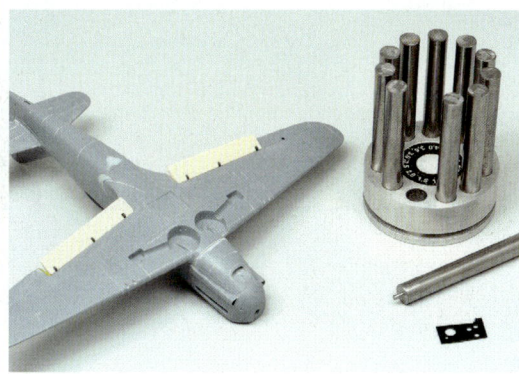

The raised panels around the guns in the wing leading edges are best reproduced with self-adhesive metal foil, trimmed to shape

Here you can see the ventral radiator unit with the new rear flap and radiator matrix details from the Brengun photo-etched set

The kit canopy is to the left (the side panels were used, as they fit perfectly) and the Falcon vac-formed one is on the right

Here you can see the side windows from the kit parts installed, along with the distinctive 'lantern' style of gunsight used by the D.520

The vac-formed windscreen was carefully attached with a little cyanoacrylate

Once all the canopy parts are ready they can be edged with thin masking tape and the remainder filled with a masking fluid like Maskol

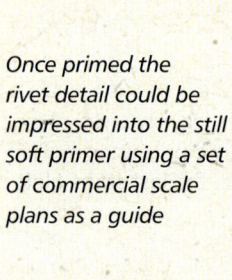

Once primed the rivet detail could be impressed into the still soft primer using a set of commercial scale plans as a guide

Any damage to the cowling panel lines was rescribed with the Hasegawa scribing tool

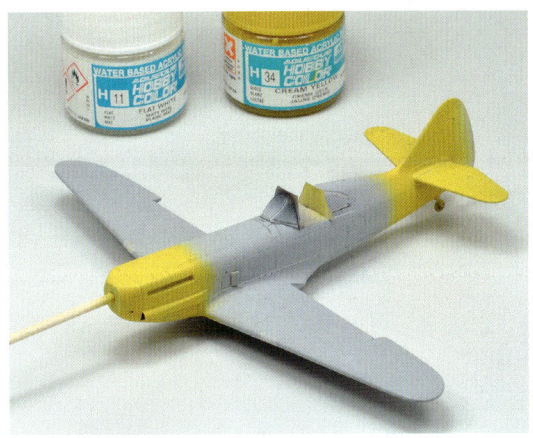

The Vichy stripes on the nose are applied with a base undercoat of white first, followed by the whole region being sprayed yellow

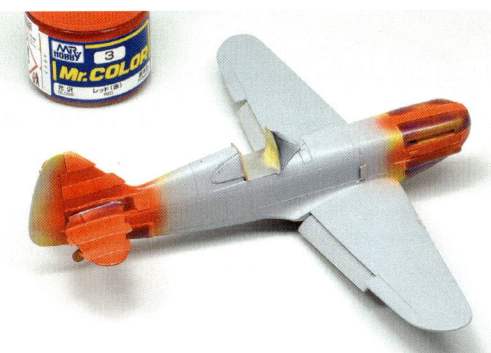

Once the white and yellow are dry, mask off the stripes to remain yellow and the red can then be applied

Take the masks off, check for any overspray or other blemishes, then the whole lot can be covered in readiness for the overall camouflage to be applied

The undersides are painted a mix of RLM 65 (H67) and FS26440 grey (H325) at a ratio of 50:50

The upper surfaces use Cocoa Brown (H17), Khaki Green (H80) and FS36320 Grey (H307)

operated by the same unit. The kit provides quite interesting schemes (at least as far as the variety of the ID stripes is concerned) for No.136 of GC II/7 based in 1942 at Sidi-Ahmed and flown by Lt Valentin, or a GC II/5 example from Casablanca flown by Lt Villacéque, I wanted a machine flown by Pierre le Gloan, the famous ace with German, Italian and British aircraft on his tally. He most probably flew the D.520 with Armée de l'Air de Vichy before he went to fly with the Allies. This machine was No.300 'White 6' belonging to GC III/6, it is not readily apparent the exact style of the stripes applied on the nose and some sources indicate that none were applied at all. However this could be caused by a combination of low contrast photographic material and poor lighting conditions for the single image of No.300 that I found in my references; or the stripes could have been added at a later date. Eventually, I decided to apply them and this is where I started painting the model. The nose and tail were primed with white (H11) followed by yellow (H24), and after masking off the individual stripes I airbrushed on red, this time from the Mr Colour range (3) which showed better opacity and usually has a harder surface than its equivalent in the Mr Aqueous Color range. Then I removed the masks, touched up any overspray or other blemishes, masked the nose and tail again with Tamiya tape and continued with the camouflage colours. The Light Blue-Grey underneath I mixed from H67 RLM 65 and H325 grey in a 50:50 ratio, while the upper colours came out of the bottles as follows: H17 Cocoa Brown, H80 Khaki Green and H307 grey all airbrushed freehand with soft transitions.

All the surfaces were sealed with GX100 gloss lacquer then I applied the decals, which were a combination of kit (insignia, tricolour stripes) and those from the older Hasegawa decal sheet (pilot's individual markings). On the wing and rudder I trimmed the excessive decals with a scalpel blade once they were sufficiently dry and touched up the edges with a corresponding shade using acrylics. Otherwise, the kit's decals performed well, they were thin, with good register and the white was opaque enough over the darkest camouflage colours. Some skill was needed, though, for precise cutting of the tricolour stripes needed for the upper parts of the landing gear doors, but the stripes were printed with sufficient margin even with potential mistakes.

Final Details

Once the landing gear components were cleaned up they were sprayed H337 Blue-Grey and with strips of Bare Metal Foil (Chrome) I added the sliding sections of each oleo leg. The doors are better replaced with photo-etched parts, which are thinner and thus looked more convincing. Attachment of the main gear legs required some guidance using a scale drawing or photograph to capture the correct angle. For the last stage I left any small items such as antenna or pitot, which I scratchbuilt from fine brass tubing. After the final matte varnish layer I airbrushed the exhaust stains using diluted black. The fuselage seemed to be quite stained with fuel and dirt around the

The decals are resilient enough to be handled and you have excess that allows you to trim around things like the rudder stripes

upper fuselage filling cap, so this was replicated with AK Production Fuel Stains applied with a fine brush and subsequently washed out a bit with MIG Productions red label thinner. The fuselage sides showed some dirt and paint scratches too, so these were gently dusted with heavily thinned sand colours and the scratches painted with Vallejo light grey-coloured acrylics.

All the various detail parts to be attached at the end, the undercarriage doors are photo-etched and the pitot and aerial mast are made from tubing

Final weathering includes paint chips applied with a fine brush using Vallejo acrylic grey

Verdict

The RS Models kit stands up well to the established, yet somewhat older Hasegawa effort that obviously offered simpler construction and overall higher quality. However, in my opinion the RS Models example looks more convincing, offering better cockpit interior and landing gear and eventually, it does not fall behind that much as far as the finesse of the surface detail goes either. Its construction is almost trouble free

and it is one of the finest RS Models efforts. The Hasegawa kit suffers from certain shape issues, though not fundamental, because the undersized radiator bath was corrected by the Hi-Tech resin item at the time, however the fuselage at the rear looks a little skinny. I can recommend this RS kit to all those modellers who have a serious interest in the type.

Paints Used
Alclad 2 lacquer:
ALC-102 Duraluminium
Gunze-Sangyo Mr Color lacquer:
C72 Intermediate Blue
C353 Zinc Chromate Yellow
C370 Azure Blue
GX100 Super Clear Gloss
Gunze-Sangyo Mr Aqueous Color acrylic:
H12 Black   H72 Dark Earth
H73 Dark Green   H309 Dark Green
Gunze-Sangyo Mr Finishing Surfacer 1500 (Black)
Gunze-Sangyo Mr Surfacer 1000 (Grey)

References
- Dewoitine D.520 by R. Danel, Profile No.135 (Profile Publications 1967)
- Dewoitine D.520 (DTU sarl 1997 ISBN: 2-912749-00-X)
- Dewoitine D.520 by W. Baczkowski (Books International 1999 ISBN: 83-906942-3-9)
- Dewoitine D.520 by B. Belcarz, Yellow Series (Mushroom Model Publications 2005 ISBN: 83-89450-09-7)
- Dewoitine D.520, Les Ailes de Gloire No.8 by P. Marchand & J. Takamori (Editions Along 2003)

Historical Significance

The French fighter industry prior to WWII was catching up with the rest of the world quite nicely, with a number of designs from different manufacturers. Amongst the best of these was the Dewoitine D.520, a sleek looking monoplane of all metal construction that had a number of advantages over the contemporary Spitfire. More internal fuel and a cannon armament made it look like it had a fine future ahead of it but the path of the War ended all hope of development as the French armed forces were battered into submission. The remaining Dewoitines, under Vichy control, made the perilous journey over to North Africa to fight for the Axis forces in their battle against the Allies. Although the French fighters were capable enough, they were severely hampered by lack of spares and trained personnel to look after them. Large numbers were lost, not only in the air campaign but also due to being under constant attack on the ground, with strafing and bombing raids on the airfields. Minor victories over the Kittyhawks and Hurricanes of the RAF and RAAF did little to hide the fact that the D.520 was a difficult aircraft to fly because of CofG problems, and not really a match for the even more modern Spitfire. When the amazing Capt Eric Brown flight-tested it, he called it "A nasty little brute!" Notwithstanding that fine description, it was also used by the Free French, the Italians, the Germans and the Bulgarians, and stayed on in post-war French service until its last flight in 1953.

- **Dewoitine D.520, '11', 1AC Escadrille Aéronavale, North Africa, March 1941**
  Vert Foncé/Terre Foncé/Gris Bleu Foncé upper surfaces and Gris Bleu Clair undersides; white arrow along fuselage sides, front of spinner; '11' on fin and outline of fuselage roundel. Standard roundels in four wing positions; unit badge aft of cockpit

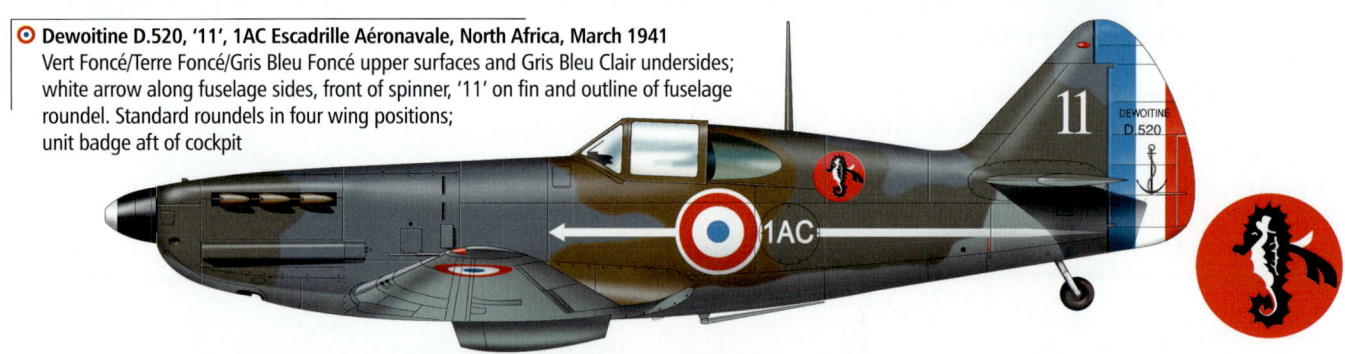

- **Dewoitine D.520, S/No.105, 'Red I' flown by Commandante Bernard Challe, 2nd Escadrille, GC I/3 based at Oran La Senia (Algeria), late 1940**
  Vert Foncé/Terre Foncé/Gris Bleu Foncé upper surfaces and Gris Bleu Clair undersides; white arrow along fuselage sides. National markings in six positions, those on fuselage outlined in white; white disc on fin with red 'I'. Unit badge on fuselage sides

- **Dewoitine D.520, S/No.471, 2 Escadrille, GCII/3 (SPA 81), Vichy Air Force, Algeria, 1942**
  Vert Foncé/Terre Foncé/Gris Bleu Foncé upper surfaces and Gris Bleu Clair undersides; yellow/red stripes around nose and rear fuselage. Yellow '28' on fuselage sides; national markings in four wing positions. Unit badge on fin; tricolour bands angled chord-wise around wings

- **Dewoitine D.520, S/No.248, 4th Escadrille, GCII/7, Vichy Air Force, Gabes (Tunisia), January 1942**
  Vert Foncé/Terre Foncé/Gris Bleu Foncé upper surfaces and Gris Bleu Clair undersides; yellow/red stripes around nose and rear fuselage. White bar along fuselage sides; national markings in six positions, bordered in white on fuselage; black disc with white '4' on fin. Red/yellow spinner, unit badge on fuselage

- **Curtiss P-40F-10, S/No.41-14268, '6', flown by Lt Legrand of 3e Escadrille, GC II/5 'Lafayette', Armée de l'Air, Souk el-Arba (Morocco), spring 1943**
  Dark Earth/Mid Stone upper surfaces with Azure Blue undersides; standard French roundels in six positions. French Blue code '6' on fuselage sides; yellow '114' on fin. Lafayette badge on fuselage sides and stork badge below windscreen

French Colour Profiles – © Richard J. Caruana 2018

- **Curtiss Hawk 75C-1 (75A-2), S/No.107, 'White 6, GC II/5 (SPA 167), Vichy Air Force, Mers el Kébir, Algeria, 1941**
  Vert Foncé/Terre Foncé/Gris Bleu Foncé upper surfaces and Gris Bleu Clair undersides; national markings in six positions, with those on fuselage sides having a white outline and horizontal bar. White '6' on fin, over a repainted patch; SPA 167 'Cicogne' emblem on rear fuselage sides

- **Curtiss Hawk 75-C1 (75A-2), S/No.179, GC II/5, Vichy Air Force, during Operation Torch, 1942**
  Vert Foncé/Terre Foncé/Gris Bleu Foncé upper surfaces and Gris Bleu Clair undersides, red/yellow stripes on engine cowling, rear fuselage and horizontal tail surfaces. National markings in six positions, with those on fuselage sides outlined in white, over a white horizontal stripe, white '7' on fuselage sides. 'Lafayette' badge on forward fuselage sides

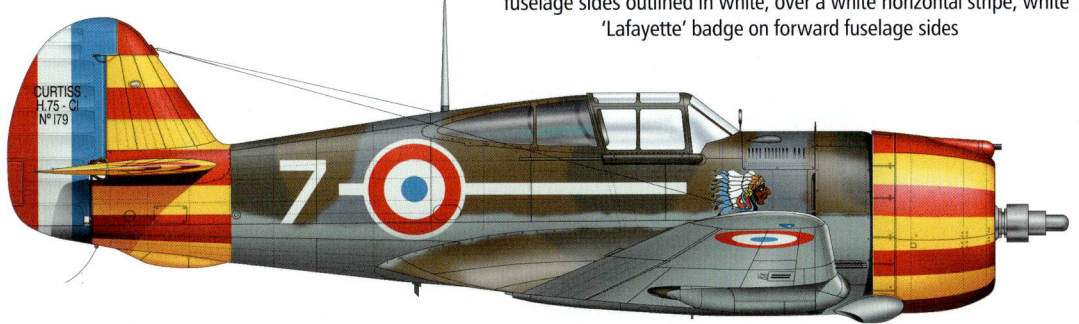

- **Bristol Blenheim Mk V, BA443, Free French Air Force, North Africa, late 1942**
  Dark Earth/Mid Stone upper surfaces with Azure Blue undersides. French roundels in four wing positions. Cross of Lorraine in red on a white disk on fuselage sides and four wing positions inboard of the roundels. Black serial

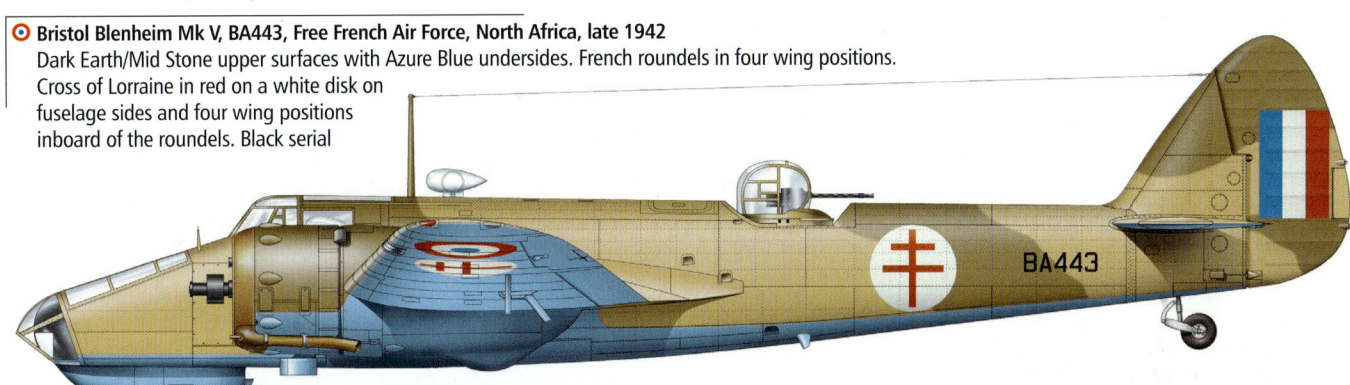

- **Lioré et Olivier LeO 451 (serial unknown), 'White 11', 2 Escadrille, GBI/22, Rabat-Salé (Morocco), summer 1942**
  TVert Foncé/Terre Foncé/Gris Bleu Foncé upper surfaces and Gris Bleu Clair undersides; red/yellow stripes around cowlings and tail. Red spinner, white '11' on fuselage sides. French roundels in four wing positions; tri-colour ribbon around wings

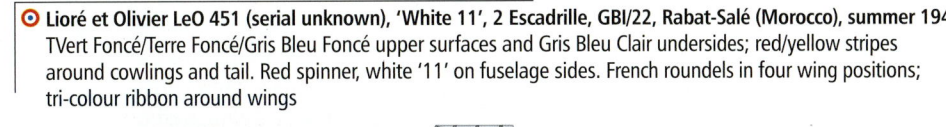
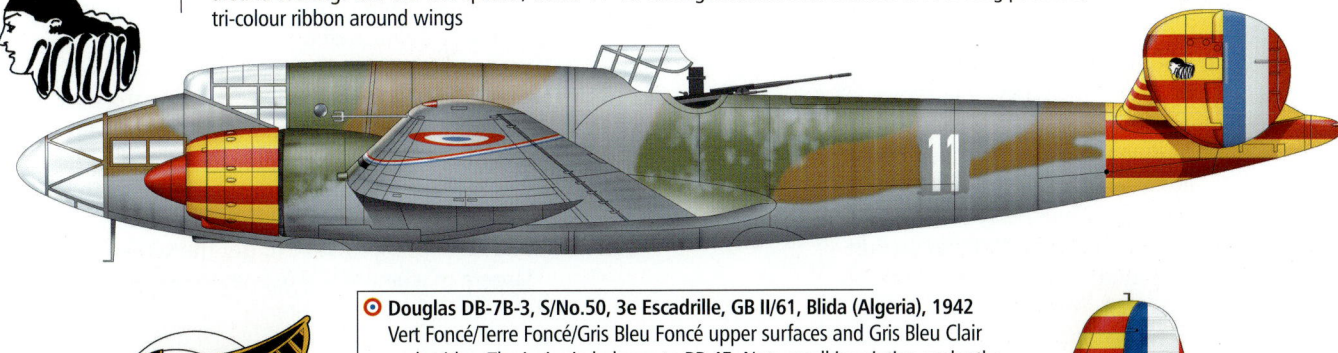

- **Douglas DB-7B-3, S/No.50, 3e Escadrille, GB II/61, Blida (Algeria), 1942**
  Vert Foncé/Terre Foncé/Gris Bleu Foncé upper surfaces and Gris Bleu Clair undersides. The insignia belongs to BR 45. Note small inscription under the badge on fin: 'Le Père'

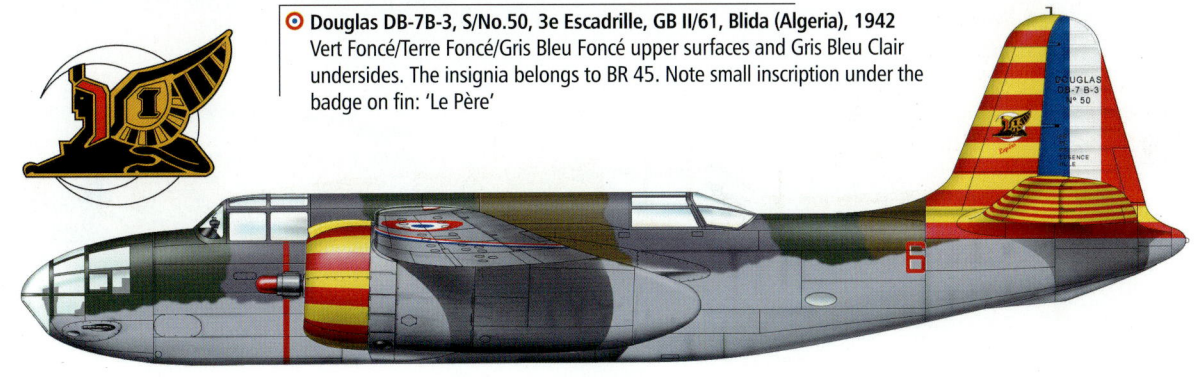

Bf 110C/E in MTO

When Eduard announced they were going to be producing a family of Messerschmitt Bf 110s for us hungry modellers, we knew we were going to get something really good. Nobody, however, expected them to be quite this complicated! As an example, in this particular box there are over 380 parts! Hiding in the rather large box with some good looking art on the lid is a selection of sprues, all in the classic Eduard olive colour. There are a huge number of unused parts as the sprues are interchangeable across the whole family of Bf 110s. That doesn't stop it being a little daunting when you first look in the box but it also looks really good. The plastic is very well done with some incredibly fine external detail and as this box is a Limited Edition version, there is also pre-painted etch and a few resin bits to play with as well. The instructions are to the usual Eduard high standard, as is the decal choice with 5 versions on offer. Thankfully, also included are the pre-cut masks for the canopy and wheels.

1/48th
by Steve A. Evans

The box is big and sturdy with a surprisingly restrained bit of art on the lid, but it's neat having the options in the box on the outside to look at before you buy

Construction

Building the machine is a tricky little process, made even more convoluted by the inclusion of pre-painted parts, so you have to get the process sequence right. Thankfully, most of the plastic bits fit very well indeed, although trial fits are recommended across the whole build. Some trimming of minor flash is needed here and there but it never gets very serious.

The cockpit looks gorgeous when it's done and so it should considering it's made up of over 80 parts! The use of both plastic and etched parts in here does create some very nice layering of the detail so it really does look the part. The pre-painted instrument panels help with this of course as the detail here is superb. The completed cockpit sub-assembly fits into the fuselage without much difficulty and when the nose is added you start to get the sense of how large a machine this must have been in real life.

Technical Data	
Eduard 1/48th Bf 110C/E in MTO	
Kit No.: 1164	Material: IM, Pe, R, Ma
Manufacturer: Eduard, Czech Republic	
UK Price: £OOP	

Talking of the nose, it's got 4 guns in it and a few bits and pieces to make it look quite realistic, although it's crying out for more wiring and extra detail. It's also designed to be left open, which I didn't want, so I stripped the guns back out and closed it all up. A sliver of 0.2mm plastic card at the aft joint did the job of taking out the irregularities of the joint and it was successfully smoothed in. Don't forget to add a couple of little blast tubes to the 20mm muzzle openings under the nose, as these are wide open on the kit, which is incorrect.

With the fuselage set aside and drying, it's time for the wings. For the most part these are trouble free, just remember to open out the holes in the lower wing for whatever stores you intend to fit. The nacelles however are not such an easy fit. These are modular assemblies, so that a number of versions can be built using the minimum number of moulds. It leads to some fit problems at the rear of the nacelle where it joins the wing. This can be minimised by trial fits and trims to get the best fit from the parts but it will still need some surgery. I found that a packer of 0.25mm plastic card positioned at the end of the nacelle and cut to shape is the best way to tidy up this troublemaker joint. Luckily, everything else fits nicely, including the interior parts for the main gear bays, with separate sidewalls and supporting struts. The detail in here is pretty good and the way it all goes together is straightforward. This is also true of the fit of the wings to the fuselage. A little trimming here and there to relieve some tight spots and they slot into place leaving no gaps at all. In fact, the fit of all the major parts can be accomplished with the minimal use of filler, which is always a good sign. Even the resin parts in the box fit very well, with only the smallest amount of preparation. You get two sets of main wheels and hubs and the tropical air filters for the intakes. The resin is beautifully cast in light grey polyurethane, without a hint of an air bubble anywhere and gorgeous detail work, so it looks like Eduard have mastered that art as well.

Talking of resin and engine nacelles, I do have one confession to make. I just couldn't face doing the exhausts on this one; 42 parts for goodness sake, and none of the stubs are hollow! I opted to spend more money and got the exhaust set QB48155 from the Quickboost range. This cut the parts count down to four and hollow cast, what's not to love? The masks were also a welcome feature as they are pre-cut to fit the canopy, so this was masked off, set into place and we were ready for paint.

Colour & Markings

In the box you get five options, all from the Mediterranean theatre of course, and all very different. There is a single Italian machine and four Luftwaffe aircraft, one desert, two in greys and one all-black night fighter. There are lots of interesting badges, a sharkmouth and beautiful looking decals for all of them. The decals include a comprehensive set of stencils as well, all in perfect register, bright colours and sharp edges. I really

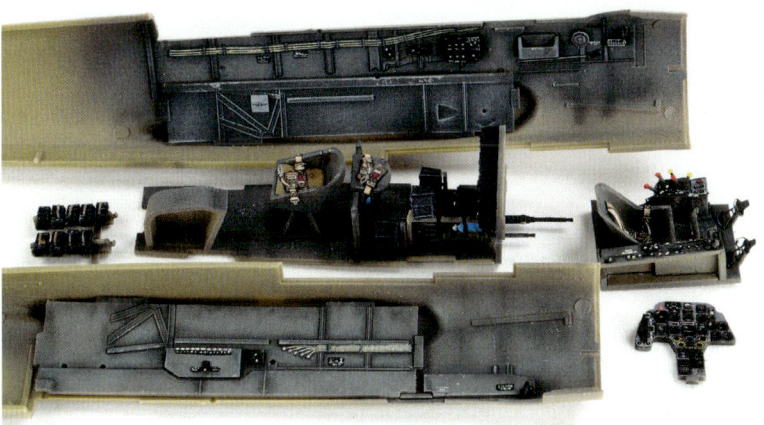

The cockpit is a marvel of modern plastic engineering. There are over 80 parts in here, so you need to up your game with the painting! The pre-painted etch for the instrument panel is lovely, though

The nose is one of the problem areas on this kit. The detail is lovely but it's designed to be left open, if you want it shut you can forget all this fiddly stuff. Note the tube additions to the nose 20mm canon muzzles

wanted a desert scheme from 7./ZG.26, which isn't included in the box, so I hunted though the spares bin and with a bit of painting for some of the letters I should get the perfect '110'.

The surface detail on the kit is extraordinarily fine, so I opted to paint this one without primer and even decided to use pre-shading to accentuate the single colours of the RLM 78/79 scheme. I also decide early on to do this one in the more fashionable style of over accentuating the shading, just to see if I like it enough to do more things that way. Pre-shading in this case was the application of semi-gloss black acrylic along the panel lines and rivet detail, with off-white areas between them. Under the following coats of paint, this should show through and different shades of the final colour. Or at least, that's the theory. The upper colour of RLM 79 Sand Brown

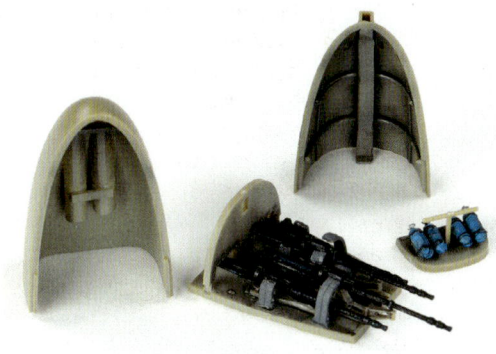

has any number of shades, depending on whom you believe, and the same goes for the underside RLM 79 Light Blue. I used Gunze-Sangyo Aqueous Hobby Colour for these and multiple coats of the base paints, as well as picking out panels and details in lighter and darker shades, accentuating the model quite nicely.

Weathering is the usual application of Tamiya Smoke, some pastel dust of various shades and then a dark brown oil wash, all sealed in under some Tamiya X22 Clear. This gloss coat makes the paint look quite dark as well as increasing the contrast of the shading but don't worry, the final surface coatings will sort that out.

The decals are a mix of the Eduard box items (including the stencils) and some from the spares box for the nose badge and basic lettering. The only one I had to paint was the white outlined 'F' on the white band. All the decals performed very

More tricky bits that need some help: the engine nacelles, the fit of these modular parts isn't the best

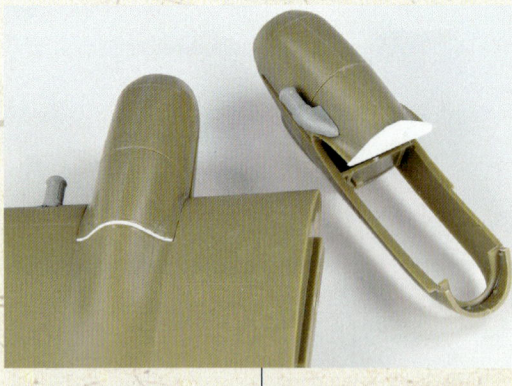

The nose cowling fitted and faired in. I like the nose profile of the 110 and really wanted this shut, so the work is a necessary evil

The fit of the wings to the fuselage is really good and the weapon tray underneath adds some very nice detail

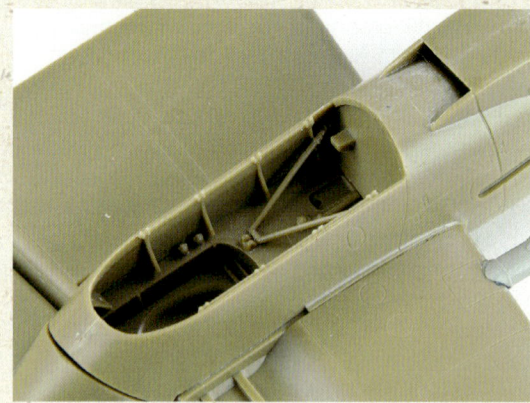

The interior of the wheel bay is very neat, although it is a little on the delicate side for such a large model

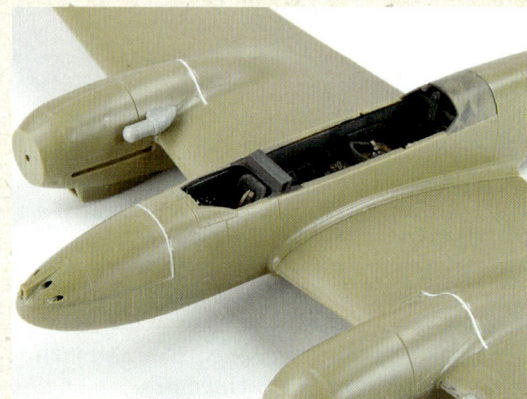

Here you can see the added plastic card pieces for the nose and nacelles, as well as the excellent resin bits in this box for the Tropical modifications

The tail, in original, small rudder form, fits very well indeed without the aid of any adjustment

Thankfully this kit comes with pre-cut masks for the greenhouse of a cockpit canopy. The masks also cover the wheels and tyres

Now here is a technique that I hardly use at all anymore: pre-shading. I opted to do this to make sure the very delicate surface details weren't covered in primer and to give me a head start on the colour

Top surface RLM 79 Sand Brown. This is the type I dark version and you can see the pre-shading has done its job, aided of course by multiple shades of the base colour being applied

This is RLM 78, or at least some version of it, although it's not clear if the Bf 110s were all repainted in this fashion

Back to the top and this is what it looked like after a couple of days of weathering with pastels. Tamiya Smoke and a few more applications of yet more shades of RLM 79

well on the gloss surface, settling down without too much hassle and leaving them with the minimum of silvering to get rid of. They are quite bright though, with the white of the national markings being particularly stark looking. This is sorted with a light dusting of grey pastel dust and a thin overspray of Tamiya Smoke, which fades it all back in rather neatly.

With markings on and dry, it's time get on with the rest of it and there's a long way to go yet.

Final Details

The undercarriage in this kit is surprisingly delicate looking. The slightly gangly looking legs and their support struts don't look, or feel, as if they will be strong enough for the finished model. It's surprising though just how sturdy it all becomes when everything is glued into place. The scissor links and actuator arms hold it all at the right angle, and with a choice of main and tail wheels it soon sits on its own feet for once. The doors are an easy fit, with positive locations on the nacelle sidewalls that were fitted earlier.

After that there are lots of the little bits to do, with aerials, pitot tubes, guns, fuel tanks and bombs. None of which is too taxing but it all takes a surprising amount of time to get right. After that it's the final coat of Xtracolor XDFF flat varnish to provide a flawless matt finish, suitable for a desert dweller like this one, before a night of drying out lets me get on with the last bits.

One bit of the jigsaw that will require plenty of attention, is the cockpit. There are a number of options in the kit, allowing you to pose the canopies open or closed, as well as different parts for different versions. The masking tape did a good job of keeping the transparent bits nice and see-through but even so, it's a shame to hide the great looking cockpit details away, so open it all up, I say. Don't forget to attach the parts with P.V.A type glues or odourless superglue to stop any fogging of the clear parts.

Ones these are in position and securely set, it's time for the last bit, the aerial wire. This particular aircraft had a single wire but some had twin aerials, one to each tail, but all had tension springs, insulator blocks and wind deflector cones, so don't leave them off or it'll look a bit naked.

Verdict

This is the third Eduard Bf 110 that I've built and I've loved each of them. It's a little tricky in places, it's got a real overkill of parts and it needs you to pay attention at all times. That's not a fault at all, it's the very nature of this kit and it's what Eduard are getting to be very good at these days, giving people the complexity that they want without having to resort to aftermarket parts for everything. This particular Limited Edition boxing

The stores for this particular model were going to be quite simple, with just the two SC500s on the centre line and auxiliary tanks under the wings. These aren't 'drop' tanks on this aircraft as they could only be removed on the ground

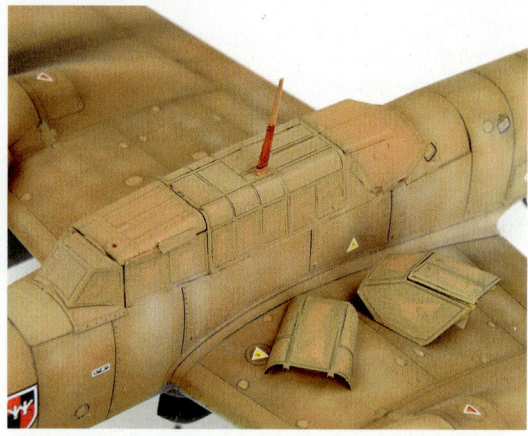

The main undercarriage bays look neat and eventually end up reasonably solid once all the bracing is in place. It was only when I was looking at this photograph that I realised I had completely forgotten the brake lines! And I call myself a professional!

The canopy looks complicated enough just masked and painted but there is a lot to do to it yet

is one of the bigger and more expensive ones but the Weekend editions are just as gorgeous, just in a more approachable format. Be prepared for doing some real work and you can look forward to having a spectacular and very commanding model on your display shelf.

Colours Used

Gunze-Sangyo Mr Aqueous Color acrylic:
H21 Off-White
H65 RLM 70 Black Green
H66 RLM 79 Sandy Brown
H70 RLM 02 Grey
H307 RLM 78 (FS36320)
H416 RLM 66 Black-Grey

This is fiddly and delicate work but it will reward you with a stunning looking model in the end. Note the single aerial wire with the deflector cone, many of these aircraft had twin wires and some none at all, it really is down to reference photos for the information

References

- Messerschmitt Bf 110 (Aero Publishers Inc.)
- Messerschmitt Bf 110, Famous Airplanes of the World No.38 (Bunrin-do)
- Messerschmitt Bf 110 by S. Nohara & S.T. Hards, Aero Detail No.21 (Dia Nippon Kaiga Co., Ltd 1998 ISBN: 4-499-22680-5)
- Messerschmitt Bf 110 At War by Armand van Ishoven (Ian Allan Ltd 1985 ISBN: 0-7110-1504-X)
- Messerschmitt Bf 110 by M. C. Windrow, Profile No.23 (Profile Publications 1965)
- Messerschmitt Bf 110 by R. Mackay (The Crowood Press 2000 ISBN: 1-86126-313-9)
- Messerschmitt Bf 110 by J, Ledwoch. Aircraft Monograph No.3 (AJ Press 1994 ISBN: 83-86208-12-0)
- Messerschmitt Bf 110 by J, Ledwoch. Monografie Lotnicze No.16 (AJ Press 1994 ISBN: 83-86208-11-2)
- Messerschmitt Bf 110: Volume 1 – C, D, E Variants by M. Lébel & P. Tomancák (Revi Publications 2009 ISBN: 80-85957-14-0) – Extremely detailed and very useful
- Messerschmitt Bf 110 Vol.I by M.J. Murawski, Monograph No.16 (Kagero 2005 ISBN: 83-89088-66-5) – Reissued 2nd edition in 2010 ISBN: 978-83-61220-52-7
- Messerschmitt Bf 110 Vol.II by M.J. Murawski, Monograph No.21 (Kagero 2005 ISBN: 83-89088-83-5)
- Messerschmitt Bf 110 Vol.III by M.J. Murawski & T. Szlagor, Monograph No.23 (Kagero 2005 ISBN: 83-89088-98-3)
- Messerschmitt Bf 110 Overall Fronts 1939-1945 by H. Nauroth & W. Held (Schiffer ISBN: 0-88740-286-0)
- Messerschmitt Bf 110C, D & E by J. Vasco & F. Estanislau (Classic Publications 2008 ISBN: 1-903223-89-5)
- Messerschmitt Bf 110 Zestörer Aces of World War 2 by J. Weal, Osprey Aircraft of the Aces No.25 (Osprey Publishing 1999)
- Messerschmitt Bf 110 Zestörer Over All Fronts 1939-1945 (Schiffer)
- Messerschmitt Bf 110 Zerstörer In Action No.30 by J.L. Campbell (Squadron/Signal Publications 1977 ISBN: 0-89747-029-X)
- Messerschmitt Bf 110/Me210/Me410: An Illustrated History by H. Mankau & P. Petrick (Schiffer ISBN: 0-7643-1784-9)
- Messerschmitt Me 110 From 1939 to 1945 by D. Breffort & A. Jouineau (Historie & Collections 2009 ISBN: 978-2-35250-144-2)

Historical Significance

The Luftwaffe Zerstörer legend was soon shown to be a bit of a myth, as we all know, but the mighty Bf 110 carried on regardless and found a multitude of uses. The campaign in North Africa was hard on both men and machines but the rugged twin took it all in its stride. Out in the expanses of the desert, the long range and safety factor of having a spare engine became very important and the Bf 110 crews came to love their aircraft. The heavy fighter soon began to be used in all sorts of ways, not only for intercepting Allied bombers and their fighter escorts but also in ground attack, light bombing and reconnaissance. The tough nature of the aircraft stood it in good stead in the harsh conditions, where the sand got into each and every crevice, while the desert sun cooked everything it touched. The ground crews loved it too because its long wing and fat nacelles made an excellent temporary sunshade during the day!

A number of operations were flown in support of the Ju 87 Stuka, as well as long missions out into the Mediterranean on convoy protection operations, all of which the Zerstörer Gruppen carried out as best they could under increasing pressure from the Allies. The big fighters handled themselves well against the bombers and early fighters such as the Gladiator, Hurricane and Kittyhawk, but when Spitfires and Mustangs started appearing more frequently, their number was up. With losses increasing, the Bf 110 was relegated to ground attack duties while the fighter missions were taken over by the newly arrived Focke-Wulf Fw 190.

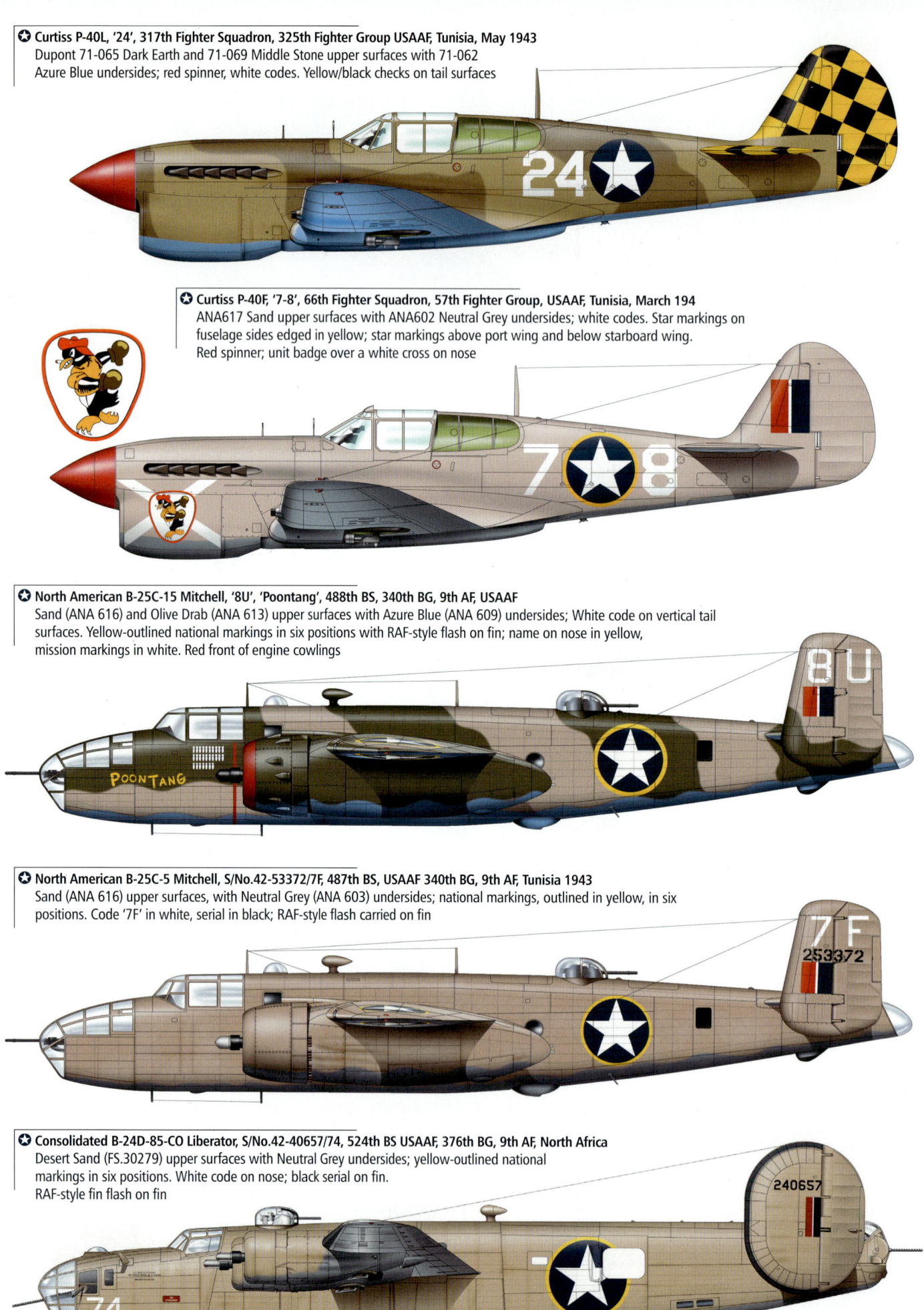

✪ **Curtiss P-40L, '24', 317th Fighter Squadron, 325th Fighter Group USAAF, Tunisia, May 1943**
Dupont 71-065 Dark Earth and 71-069 Middle Stone upper surfaces with 71-062 Azure Blue undersides; red spinner, white codes. Yellow/black checks on tail surfaces

✪ **Curtiss P-40F, '7-8', 66th Fighter Squadron, 57th Fighter Group, USAAF, Tunisia, March 194**
ANA617 Sand upper surfaces with ANA602 Neutral Grey undersides; white codes. Star markings on fuselage sides edged in yellow; star markings above port wing and below starboard wing. Red spinner; unit badge over a white cross on nose

✪ **North American B-25C-15 Mitchell, '8U', 'Poontang', 488th BS, 340th BG, 9th AF, USAAF**
Sand (ANA 616) and Olive Drab (ANA 613) upper surfaces with Azure Blue (ANA 609) undersides; White code on vertical tail surfaces. Yellow-outlined national markings in six positions with RAF-style flash on fin; name on nose in yellow, mission markings in white. Red front of engine cowlings

✪ **North American B-25C-5 Mitchell, S/No.42-53372/7F, 487th BS, USAAF 340th BG, 9th AF, Tunisia 1943**
Sand (ANA 616) upper surfaces, with Neutral Grey (ANA 603) undersides; national markings, outlined in yellow, in six positions. Code '7F' in white, serial in black; RAF-style flash carried on fin

✪ **Consolidated B-24D-85-CO Liberator, S/No.42-40657/74, 524th BS USAAF, 376th BG, 9th AF, North Africa**
Desert Sand (FS.30279) upper surfaces with Neutral Grey undersides; yellow-outlined national markings in six positions. White code on nose; black serial on fin.
RAF-style fin flash on fin

USAAF Colour Profiles – © Richard J. Caruana 2018

✪ **Douglas A-20B, S/No.41-3241/36 of the 47th BG, USAAF, Souk-el-Arba (Tunisia), May 1943**
Sand upper surfaces while undersides remain Neutral Grey. White codes, yellow serial.
Area around nose patched up, probably covering a previous identity or nose art

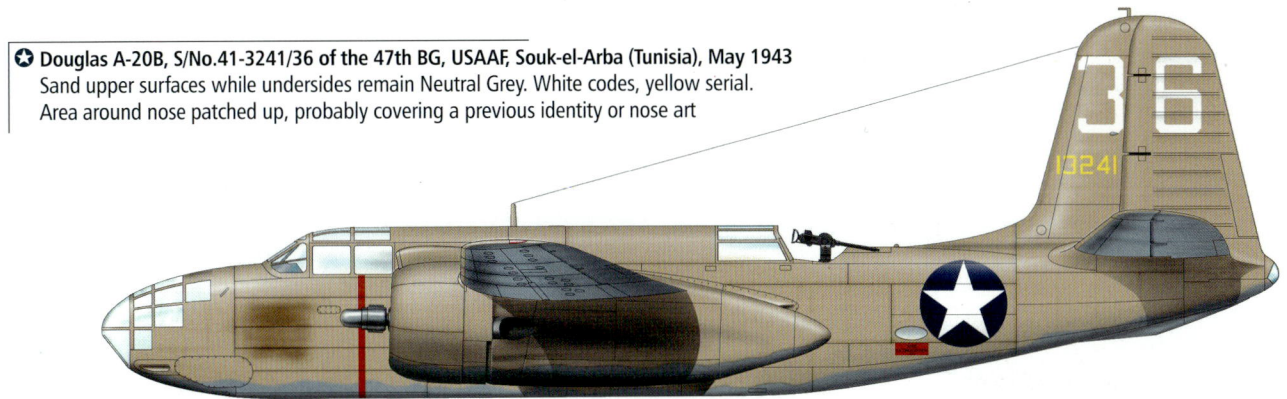

✪ **Boeing B-17F-25-BO, S/No.41-24571, 'Indianapolis Warbird', 49th BS, 2nd BG, 15th AF USAAF, Tunisia, summer 1943**
Olive Drab with dabbling of Medium Green upper surfaces; Neutral Grey undersides. Name on nose and serial on fin in yellow. National markings with red surround on fuselage sides, above port and below starboard wings.
Unit markings in white on fin

✪ **Supermarine Spitfire Mk Vb, ER120/VF-D, 5th Fighter Squadron, 52nd FG USAAF, Operation Torch, November 1942**
Dark Earth/Mid Stone upper surfaces with Azure Blue undersides; white codes and black serial. RAF markings painted over; US star markings on fuselage sides, above port and below starboard wing, outlined in yellow. Red spinner; US flag on fuselage, aft of cockpit

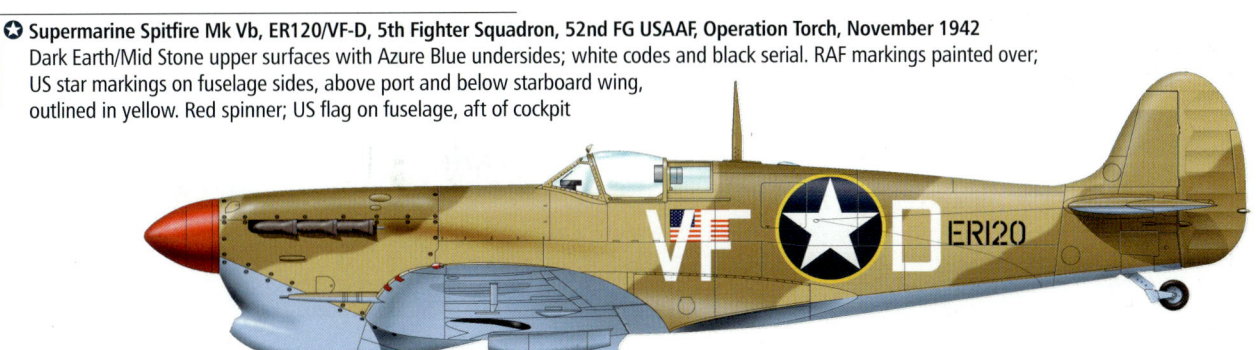

✪ **Supermarine Spitfire Mk Vb, ER256/FMD, flown by Colonel Fred M. Dean, Commander of the 31st FG USAAF, Tunisia, 1943**
Dark Earth/Mid-Stone/Azure Blue finish with red spinner. Codes in white (serial partially overpainted).
Note that the code letters are, in fact, the pilot's initials and not those of the Group

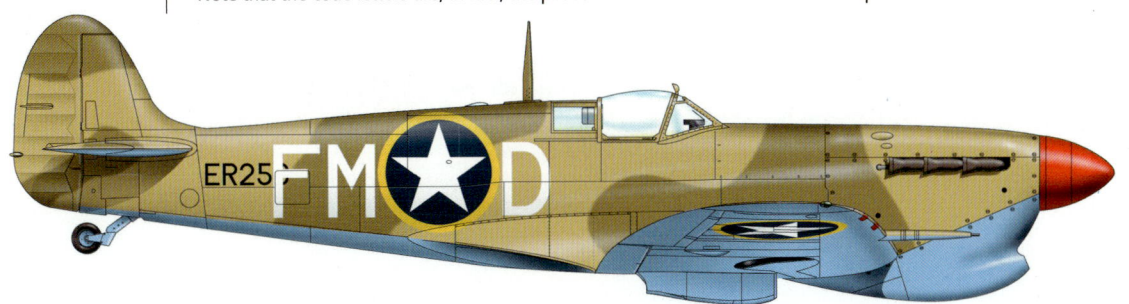

✪ **Supermarine Spitfire Mk IXc, EN307, 307th Fighter Squadron, 31st Fighter Group, 12th Air Force USAAF, Tunisia, 1943**
Dark Earth and Mid Stone upper surfaces with Azure Blue undersides.
Codes in white, serial in black. National markings on fuselage sides,
above port and below starboard wings

✪ **Lockheed P-38H-5-LO Lightning, 'White 70', 1st FG USAAF, 2nd AF, North Africa, 1943**
Olive Drab upper surfaces with patches of Medium Green applied to edges of flying surfaces (including fin/rudder); Neutral Grey undersides. Mid-blue nose and fuselage bands; white '70'. National markings above port and below starboard wings

✪ **North American P-51 Mustang, S/No.41-37322, 154th Observation Squadron, USAAF, French North Africa, 1942**
Olive Drab upper surfaces with Neutral Grey undersides. Yellow codes, wing/tailplane bands and name 'Mah Sweet – Eva Lee' on nose. Red Spinner. Gas detection patches aft of cockpit and on fin. 48-star US flag on vertical tail surfaces. National markings, with yellow surround, on fuselage sides, above port and below starboard wings

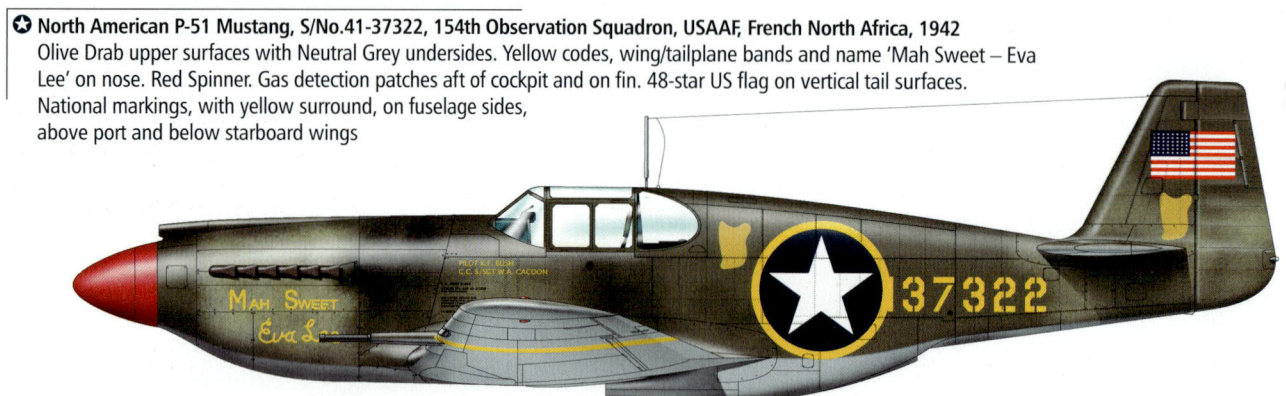

✪ **Bell P-400 Airacobra, 24520/V, X-R, 'Evelyn', 346th FS USAAF, 350th FG, North Africa, early summer 1943**
Basic RAF Dark Earth/Dark Green/Sky finish with red spinner; Olive Drab front fuselage panel, possibly from another aircraft. Codes and serial in yellow; US Star outlined in red (May to June 1943) on fuselage sides, above port and below starboard wings. Note RAF serial overpainted in light grey under elevators; some sources quote fuselage band in yellow, though the regulation Sky is probably more than likely

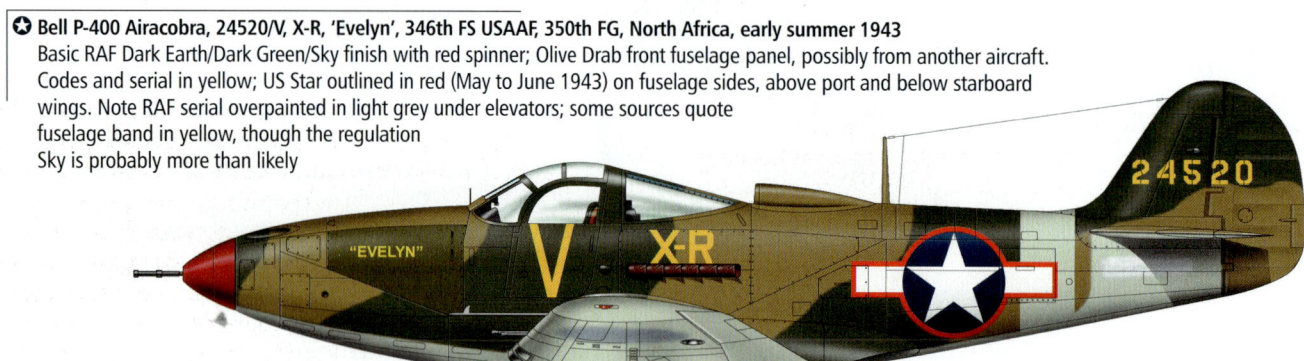

✪ **Piper L-4, S/No.42-36389, USAAF, Operation Torch, North Africa, 1942**
Olive Drab/Neutral Grey scheme with yellow engine cowling and serial; US star markings, outlined in yellow, in standard positions

✪ **Grumman F4F-4 Wildcat, 29-GF-10, VGF-29, USS Santee (CVE 29), Operation Torch, November 1942**
Non-specular Blue/Grey upper surfaces; Non-specular Light Grey undersides. Star markings with wide yellow border in six positions. Code is black and white

USAAF Colour Profiles – © Richard J. Caruana 2018 — Airframe Extra No.9 – North Africa Campaign